STARS OF BURMA

and

POEMS ON THE THEME OF WAR

ISBN 1 897 887 53 1

Published by:
Natula Publications
5 St Margarets Avenue, Christchurch, Dorset BH23 1JD
email: info@natula.co.uk

The *Stars of Burma* poem was originally published privately by the author in 1997.

British Library Cataloguing-in-Publication Data.
A catalogue record for this book is available from the British Library.

Printed by Impress Print, Corby, Northamptonshire NN18 8EW

The publishers would like to thank the Imperial War Museum, London for their permission in using photographs from their collections.

Front Cover Illustration: The Only Spoon
Back Cover Illustrations: **Centre** - 'Stilwell's Road' through the jungle
Back Cover Illustrations: **Surround** – Insignia of some the Regiments who fought during the Burma Campaign.

The Viscount Slim

House of Lords

11th September 1997

Mrs Kathleen Ross
18 Exton Road
Boscombe East
Bournemouth
Dorset BH6 5QF

Dear Mrs. Ross,

How kind and thoughtful of you to send me a copy of your poem Stars of Burma. Thank you.

I am about to go to America on a Burma Star Association visit, so will read the peom in the aeroplane.

My congratulations to you, and all good wishes from me and all of us in the Burma Star.

Yours sincerely

John Slim

MY THANKS TO

Dr Robin Philipp of the Department of Occupational Medicine, Bristol Royal Infirmary. We have been in touch since 1995, after which time he has formed Lapidus based on the theory of 'using words to help with our health'. Lapidus is now funded by the Arts Council and has been a wonderful mainstay in my life.

Alison Combes, Education Development Officer, 1995; Christine Hall of Poetry Please, 1995; Alan Milburn M.P., Health Minister, 2003; The Viscount Slim; Nigel Steel, Department of Documents, Imperial War Museum; The Salamander Oasis Trust; The Burma Star Association who have all supported me.

All the doctors, surgeons and nurses in hospitals who asked for a poem; my surgeon, Mr Blakeway, at the Royal Bournemouth Hospital whose skill has enabled me to move from my desk and Sister who said, "I have never had a patient with such a vivid imagination as you, Kathleen!"

Rose Waldren for her typing and help over the years, Jane Martin of Natula Publications whom I cannot thank enough, and my daughters, albeit in Spain, Australia and the Isle of Wight.

All those kind recipients of my poems who took the time to write appreciative letters and which gave me the inspiration to write these poems: HRH Prince of Wales; HRH Princess Anne; HRH Princess Diana; Rt. Hon. Lord Healey of Riddlesden; Lord Montagu of Beaulieu; Lieut. Commander C.P. Addis RN, HMS Victory; Mary O'Hara, singer; Christopher Peacock, Southern TV; Eric Newby, *The Observer*; Anne Forty, The Bovington Tank Museum and the Bournemouth Samaritans.

Writers and fellow poets who have offered me advice and encouragement: Samuel Hynes; Carol Easton; Ian Bradley, Professor at New College Oxford; Michael Rosen; the late Thomas Blackburn; Dannie Abse; Pam Ayres; John Brown of BBC Radio London, Poetry Dept.; especially Lotte Kramer, who gratefully received the dedication to *Black Dogs of the World* and said that the poem 'is packed with ideas and very thought provoking' and Edward Storey who sent me a poem about a poet 'from one poet to another'.

And last but not least, all those wonderful veterans who shared, if somewhat reluctantly, some of their war experiences. I salute them.

DEDICATION

For my Parents

Percival Howard

and

Alice Maud Preston

With all my love and gratitude

Kathleen Ross

THE AUTHOR

Kathleen Ross was born in Bexhill-on-Sea, Sussex, in 1916 and educated at Bexhill Secondary School. On her 17th birthday she enrolled to train as a State Registered Children's Nurse at Queen Mary's Hospital for Children, Carshalton, Surrey. In 1937 as a SRCN she transferred to Hammersmith Hospital, London. Kathleen married at the onset of war and over the years had six daughters. She has been widowed for 25 years and now lives in Bournemouth.

Having worked in some of the largest mental hospitals on night duty, Kathleen saw the advent of the 'un-locked doors' policy at Graylingwell Hospital, Sussex. She began writing poetry seriously while confined to a wheelchair for many years following an accident when coming off night duty.

Kathleen has written a series of War, Dissident, Nursing, Romantic, Children's and Religious poems. Some of her poems have appeared in magazines and she has letters from many famous people, Yehudi Menhuin for example, to whom she has sent poems.

She has written a novel, prompted by the publishers Hutchinson who showed an interest in her work after reading one of her poems. She is currently involved in a project 'Poetry as Therapy' in the Art of Medicine pioneered by Dr Robin Philipp, Bristol Royal Infirmary, for the World Health Organisation.

Stars of Burma was inspired by the wonderful spirit shown in the Campaign, and was written while spending many weeks in leg plaster casts after six knee operations. "I knew my suffering was nil compared to that endured by the men and women involved in this most epic struggle."

Kathleen hopes that any profits from her book of poems including *Stars of Burma*, an epic of 8,000 words dedicated to 'The Forgotten Army' and Lord Louis Mountbatten, will help the veterans and their families. *Stars of Burma* is currently archived and is on view to the general public in the Burma Corner of the Imperial War Museum, Lambeth Road, London SE1 6HZ.

INTRODUCTION

War was the backdrop of my life as a small child born in 1916 when my father was a P.O.W. and my earliest memories are of the officers billeted in our house. They had very white teeth, laughed a great deal and fed me delicious chocolate. When my father returned he had blackened teeth, frowned a lot and had only a few wispy strands of hair. He was very thin and pale and I apparently drew away from his embrace and cried, "I don't like you!" How I must have wounded his feelings with that tactless childish remark but I think he eventually forgave me.

My father suffered from agoraphobia but he tried to regain his health and build a business up from scratch, as my mother was pregnant. I would take my homework and 'mind the shop' while he went next door to the barbers for a shave and haircut.

Every Sunday before dinner, he would retire to his bedroom and I would take up his meal, which was sometimes hurled out of the bedroom window. I can still remember the roast beef, potatoes and cabbage with gravy splattered over the grass amongst the pieces of shattered china. Our beloved cat would joyously approach this unexpected feast and I was pleased it wasn't wasted.

My youngest sister, who joined up for the ATS in World War II, was at home with my parents when Winston Churchill gave his War Declaration Speech to the nation on the wireless in 1939. She told me recently of our father's reaction when he listened to the news that we were at war with Germany. She said that he burst into tears and rushed upstairs to shut himself in his bedroom. The trauma he received when he was a young man as the result of his experiences as a soldier and prisoner of war in World War I never left him.

Then down came the backdrop of war again. As a young mother, my war was not one that required me to kill the enemy although I did fill a kettle with water ready to switch it on to boil, and which I stood at an open bedroom window. The idea was to pour it onto the head of any invading German soldier who might be standing underneath in the little porch. This indicates how fiercely the average civilians would use any means to defend their homeland. We did shelter child refugees who had escaped over the Pyrenees and also gave priests and the odd soldier a few quietish nights' rest although the gun site on Wimbledon Common nearby was very loud and food scarce. This caused a Canadian officer to remark, "Gee ma'am, you civilians have it worse than the front!" but I knew this was an exaggeration. I liked the meagre rations because I kept my slim figure.

We ignored the air raid sirens as we sat in the local cinema and forgot the war especially with the lovely film *Wuthering Heights*; there was always the radio with Winston Churchill's speeches.

For safety I went to South Wales in a troop train with two small children under five and I was six months pregnant. On arrival the city of Swansea had been badly bombed and my husband's relatives were unable to take me in. I lived in a primitive cottage until it was obvious that there were no facilities for me to have the baby. I must have been one of the few pregnant evacuee mothers to have her fare paid to get back to London to have the baby. I was only able to stay in hospital for the actual birth and on returning home to Wimbledon had a bad attack of shingles. It was at this time that the 'doodle bugs' and then the V2 rockets began to appear over England.

For the children's sake we slept in the cold and dirty coal cellar at night and in the morning would collect the pieces of flak which had fallen from the dog fights overhead, to be returned for the war effort. We queued for our rations, sometimes stepping on broken glass from shattered shop windows. My first three daughters, born to the loud roar of the guns, were being taken for an airing on Wimbledon Common when I saw what I knew to be my first 'doodle bug'. I made up a game about a very fierce bird, and we all jumped into a ditch, emerging when we heard a bang in the not too far distance.

The anniversary of VE Day and at last our war debt is over. As Britain celebrates the 60th anniversary of victory over Germany the government is finally preparing to pay the last of the war debt owed to the United States. The Imperial War Museum is setting up an 'adopt a veteran' scheme in which old soldiers go into schools to talk to pupils about their experiences.

Published to commemorate the 60th anniversary of the end of the Second World War, this book is a collection of poems, written by an ordinary woman born during the First World War, and broadly covers the 20th century wars, illustrating their effects on different people and places.

Finally, whilst I have received unstinting support and advice in writing this book of poems, I apologise for any errors or omissions that may remain.

Kathleen Ross
May 2005

CONTENTS

Poems

CONTENTS (Continued)

CONTENTS (Continued)

CONTENTS (Continued)

THE BRIDGE

An army crawls on jungle road,
An army of retreat;
If men fall out with their heavy load
They'll not regain their feet.

Torn ribboned shirt from jungle thorn
Striped black with staining wet;
Eyes red rimmed, stiff matted beards worn
Caked white, with salty sweat.

Overhead dust floats in a cloud
Dry settles on the ground;
The parched mouths cannot speak aloud
Where footfalls make no sound.

Both bombed and gunned the Burma coast
Is broken flank to rear;
And roadblocks' fire like Hamlet's ghost
Of father, fans their fear.

Like sleepwalkers' dread nightmares tire
As urge and goad them on;
To Sittang Bridge they must retire
Slim thread of steel and stone.

The enemy on land and sea
In undiscloséd strength;
May seize the bridge so they must flee
Along its slender length.

Leader, Major General Smyth
Seventeenth Division;
Finds hope as dusk begins to rise,
Can cross, with all provision?

At three a.m. upon the bridge
A lorry overturned;
The Japanese upon the ridge
Invaded as they burned.

The fear, must blow the bridge, at last
Became a ghastly fact;
The centre span destroy by blast
The only way to act?

At this the silence was profound,
Then excited chatter;
On Mokpalin above the ground
Great hail of bullets spatter.

Our soldiers stripped of clothes, so tired
They sank unarmed in mud;
Some shot as enemy fast fired
While others drowned in flood.

All men who reached the other side
Collapsed in weary pain;
In agony endured the ride
Borne slow on Burma train.

The cost was high yet something saved
They evacuate Rangoon;
Through jungle, swamp and sand, they braved
The hills that housed monsoon.

These units of a rearguard fight
Where heroes are unspoken;
These shattered remnants lived in right
Battered, but unbroken.

Cut roads on cliffs on mountain wall
Soaked through with clouds of rain;
At India's frontier marched long haul
Unconquered, rose again.

THE SHIELD OF INDIA

With forefinger that southward points
So Burma's like a hand;
Where mountains range like finger joints
From strange and savage land.

Here three long rivers twist and roam
The world's roof, resting there;
Bare desolate and lonely home
Of llamas, panda bear.

Its barrier a natural shield
The enemy now breached;
Their conquest piled, swift sword they wield
And Singapore they reached.

With force and speed, like rushing bore
They storm the Burmese vales;
And British-Chinese forces tore
Like oak tree's branch in gales.

But from the North a new road built,
Another airline made;
Avenging for Pearl Harbour's guilt
Now, retribution paid.

To India the British turned,
The Chinese to Yunnan;
The Allies derrick oilfields burned,
And flames of petrol fan.

Green paddy fields in peaceful times
Grew many tons of rice;
Soft are the valleys' temperate climes -
A bounty beyond price.

The inner basin had two gains
The Japanese knew well;
Lessened were malaria's pains
And monsoon's drenching hell.

The Southern zone was sheltered and
The wind and rain veered round;
Communications they command
Were better on the ground.

The Eastern front we thinly manned
As lacked supporting gear;
Good air support was not yet planned
At Christmas of that year.

BURMA FALLS

The enemy were quick to come
As Christmas Day dawned clear;
Victoria Point at first they won -
Bombed Rangoon, fostered fear.

In from Siam East they struck
Tovay was overcome;
All roads and railways North, they cut
Our troops were on the run.

Were ferried fast in various boat
So reached to Martaban;
Civilian crews kept them afloat
Showed courage, every man.

The Koylies and the Gurkhas held
The line behind Belin;
Though enemy's great strength repelled
At Sittang hemmed them in.

And Stuart carriers and tanks
Drew alongside at the quays;
A weary army owe their thanks
To such brave men as these.

North to India all the way
These tanks an army saved;
They held Jap armoury at bay
As obstacles they braved.

So land links broke as Burma fell
With Rangoon thus destroyed;
All sea power lost so Stilwell
Joined, and Chinese troops employed.

Chiang Kai-shek, came forth with aid
The enemy to know;
Caustic, craggy as they're made
Was leader, Uncle Joe.

O.B.O.A. Command then failed
Though Gloucester tanks oppose;
As Japs their swords unceasing flailed,
Black cloud o'er Syrian, rose.

At Prome, Lieutenant General Slim
Stood firm as rock, he said;
That later he'd take troops to win
As back through Burma, led.

The enemy's strong air power fought
To win them every fight;
And thus a lesson we were taught
As through the fires took flight.

To win a victory well armed
Need power in the air;
This the first factor to command
Or else, all is despair.

For now the patriots could turn
And infiltrate the land;
To loot, and kill, and snipe, and burn
In vicious roving band.

So fire and flames swept over where
Pergodas, temples, all;
Like red umbrella, flame and flare
As one by one, they fall.

The Chinese troops were beaten back
Half way to Mandalay;
Where oilfields were destroyed by flak,
It was the only way.

For two days desperate battle fought
As sun blazed fiery red;
The Chinese, Scots and Indians caught
With British, forged ahead.

Lifeline to Irrawaddy saved
Our troops were free again;
They poured in thousands as they braved
Where mules screamed, mad with pain.

Disaster fell on other flank
As spearhead held at bay;
At Chindwin sappers manned the bank
Far south at Mandalay.

Two spans of Ava Bridge, they blew,
In nightmare stumbled slow;
As weakened, wounded, worse it grew
On bleeding feet to go.

At this same place at later date
Our army would return;
A mammoth Bailey bridge to make
Where tanks and stores now burn.

So out of Burma Stilwell went
Emerged at Homalin;
Led only armed with stick unbent
Where mountains hemmed them in.

The Tamu road was left behind
Washed clean by monsoon rain;
These humid drenching heights thus climbed
Consolidate, again.

To Myitkyina then they came
These victors from Japan;
Who struck through mangrove swamps, to run
And Ramree Island, man.

So one last plane from Burma flew
With Governor aboard;
In India he could review
And weary troops applaud.

From Burma where the lawless, loot
Two thousand wounded, took;
With courage tracked that trackless route
Forward, not backward, look.

LEAN DAYS

Still under arms with men from home
Enduring pouring rain;
These regiments of skin and bone
Made Japanese abstain.

The wheel deep mud they could not face
Against such fighting force;
Whose training for this alien place.
Was of too short a course.

Invasion took its dreadful fees
As enemies transpire;
Two hundred thousand refugees
Fled fast from sword and fire.

This exodus of every age
Was ruled by vicious force;
Disease and rumour, rife, rampage
So, martial law, enforce.

Communications were but few,
Dread Hukawing a trap;
This valley, the dead, only knew
In its green mantle, wrap.

Now, two-way traffic was devised
The highest peaks to span;
Across the 'Hump' flew planes comprised
To ferry fighting man.

No joy ride this, but dangerous
Strong turbulence could spell;
To make all fear superfluous
Drop plane like stone down well.

Planes plied the skies, to China flew
On shuttle run they flowed;
From skeleton this ferry grew
As big achievement showed.

Force X and Y in battle skills
These Chinese troops so named;
As General Stilwell warded ills
The Japanese proclaimed.

The Yunnan project - late the length
Of Ledo Road not built;
So Wavell distributed strength
On coastline, stretched to hilt.

Along Brahmaputra Vale
Maintaining force was made;
On ever growing ground entail
Where chain of airfields laid.

This golden bridge to China dream
An architect might plan;
Projected General Arnold's scheme
Ohio to Assam.

Four thousand miles strategic, plays
Important part to place;
These were the lean and hungry days
Build hospital and base.

Land roads in Manipur not wait
While Assam floods were drained;
Abortive, fail to infiltrate
So, Malay, not reclaimed.

The thrust to Akyab was held
Wingate had no relief;
Experiments, whose failures spelt
A lesson full of grief.

REPULSE IN ARAKAN

In this first Arakan campaign
Land full of many ills;
So narrow was the bare terrain
Of jungle covered hills.

Of swamps, and paddy fields, and scrub
Where enemy low hide;
Tanks fail assault in crumbling mud
Where flats are crossed by tide.

For Japanese supplies and men
With Foul Point at its tip;
Their island garrison was then
By Mayu Range, steep split.

The port of Akyab lay South
Of India Burma line;
For creeks and gullies at its mouth
Assault craft's best design.

But these amphibious boats were short
But Wavell thrust by land;
At Donbaik his troops were caught
By enemy at hand.

The British Indian Brigade
Not luckless pattern, change;
As Japs their reinforcements made
Gunned - mortared - at close range.

Japs forced our flank to alter course
To scatter and to flee;
As led by a dynamic force
Colonel Tanahashi.

At Rathedung when fierce they struck,
First Punjab's fire broke out;
Charged bayonets-swept Japs amok
O'er paddy fields in rout.

Lieutenant Colonel Lowther sat
In deckchair, drinking tea;
And from this vantage point could map
The moves of enemy.

But Tanahashi's claws still gripped
As straddled Mayu Range;
The Sixth Brigade was soundly whipped,
As his patrols arrange.

For failure to organise,
Wavell made his reply;
"The task I set to finalise
Caused many men to die."

When element of swift surprise
From tactics, disappeared;
The enemy then realise
Their main content, not feared.

Two other factors contribute
To enemy's great strength;
The Infantry's strong attribute
Was march of fearful length.

Fanatic bravery they showed -
For answer, this we knew;
By Arakan's wet coastal road
Build airstrip straight and true.

To fill our troops with confidence
In leaders, tactics, arms;
Joined with belief in Providence,
Slim's hard work, calmed all qualms.

This dynamo all armies need
In which to place their trust;
Such discipline of faith, to lead
To march, and fight, and thrust.

The Hurricanes and Zeros fought,
But R.A.F. was lost;
The enemy a mixture sought
To win at any cost.

At Chittagong, Dohazari
Our fighters bombed on land;
Straffed o'er Comilla and Feni
As mastery they planned.

But Japanese air power we gripped -
Offensive was repelled;
As R.A.F. offset and whipped
To shoot as fast they shelled.

With Indians and British flew
Americans, fast fly;
As army of the jungle grew
Were spreading wings on high.

The jungle war with power in air
We revolutionised;
Thus enemy, foul means or fair
Employed, as planes surprised.

The Allies started all from scratch
Fought dust and mud, and heat;
Brick, oil, and concrete on which latch
And nature's effort, beat.

Now air support was very strong
And ready to attack;
From hard retreat so cruel and long
Now, shape the sweet way back.

Four special duties on air, laid -
The wounded must transport;
Direct attack on front line made -
Supplies bring for support.

As enemy's transport disrupt
Is bombed both day and night;
With flashing fire these bombs erupt -
On Bangkok glowed their light.

FIRST MISSION

A powerful mind, of late, whose fate
In forty two, to show;
Was Major General Wingate
Who held the D.S.O.

He struck alone, his Chindits formed
River Chindwin, crossing;
Such bravery their deeds performed,
In history, will sing.

The second phase now took its place
The Irrawaddy cross;
Communications to displace
Fire dumps, add every loss.

The Mandalay-Lashio raid
Defeated him at last;
For heat and thirst their mark they made
And so the die was cast.

At least a thousand miles each marched
O'er mass of formless hills;
Accomplished in ten weeks, as parched
And weak, they stretched their wills.

The Burmese troops as guides, were brave
With skills in jungle fight;
Our success measured, for we have
Great qualities of might.

In warfare ancestor possessed
Intelligence undimmed;
Had power to give of his best
When audience was thinned.

Original in lonely place
As on himself rely;
The British soldier war will face
With moral courage high.

Thus General Wingate made this claim
"So limited the mind
Of Japanese, whose sole great aim,
Is copy all his kind."

"The unexpected made him hate,
Withdrew in baffled rage;
And obstinate and angry wait
For could not battle wage."

THE BIRTH OF S.E.A.C.

Resilience, the army found
In nineteen forty three,
Gave men patrolling on the ground
Superiority.

With 'man to man' as number grew
Offensives were well led;
Gave high success when army knew
Great confidence was bred.

In South East Asia, born to lead
Mountbatten was first choice;
And more great names we heard to heed
Joined in victory voice.

'Speck' Wheeler organised supplies
Administered with flair;
American and Anglo lives
Were integrated there.

Administration operate
This Auchinleck, did pen;
With India co-operate
Count, two million men.

The Indian railway now address
Supplies were its first aim;
Transport was vital, so they press.
New method - speed its claim.

A highway built from Dimapur
As roads were mechanised;
In first stage of the Ledo Spur -
Then China organise.

So India's frontiers we kept
As over 'Hump' we fly;
Marched, fought, and flew as monsoon wept -
From fever did not die.

"Like drawing stumps at cricket match
In rain," let monsoon flood;
Flow unexpected, floored the Japs
Who could not face the mud.

Then fighting spirit rose, as when,
Where Japs no longer hide;
Upon a box, before his men
Mountbatten did confide...

"Their Emperor is God the one
Before they all must bow;
They nature fight, as drugs have none
Intelligence is low."

"Communications Japs may split
But our airdrop, defeat;
Stay put, the enemy, we'll hit
There'll be no more retreat."

And so troops fighting spirit grew
As torrents on them rained;
Through monsoon marched, and fought, and flew
Malaria, contained.

Large air supply was dropped with ease
As Kabaw Valley hold;
Good news of War, the troops to please
Their special paper, told.

Thus parachuted from on high
Advances to report;
In nineteen forty four, reply
In Arakan, we fought.

SECOND ATTACK FROM ARAKAN

The Jap conquest their limit take
Advancing to secure;
To India the bases break -
Initiative is poor.

Assault craft now, could not be found
Mountbatten's plan was spoiled;
So into Burma marched on ground,
And Japanese were foiled.

Across the mountain Stilwell veered
To Myitkyina;
In Arakan, Slim pushed and cleared
Mayu Peninsular.

The River Naaf for sea supply -
On metal highway load;
Where Mayu Range is tunnelled by
Maung-daw-Buthidaung Road.

Important were the tunnels sought
To contact near or far;
As Japanese from buttress fought
Bombing worst in Burma.

Beyond the mass of hills Slim went
Both sides of Mayu Range;
Here, the transport squadrons sent
Where left flank could exchange.

And 'Mother Bird' bore mail and food
By Africans esteemed;
This wonderful approach was good
Beyond their wildest dreams.

So enemy diverted force
Against the valley guard;
As this intrigue depleted source
Their plans could not safeguard.

Now, Ngakyedauk hailed -
Mere mule tracks cut the gorge;
As India's invasion failed
The Eighty-Ninth now forge.

The miners and the sappers strove
To make the road they need;
Pneumatic drills to use bulldoze -
New records set for speed.

Christison now, began his thrust
Of movement, straight ahead;
The Infantry in clouds of dust
With motor transport, thread.

By foothill's scrub and stunted trees
'Three Jolly Japs', small inn;
A hillock, horseshoe shaped, to please
Where all were deep dug in.

The British guns and mortars, poise
Defences disappeared;
'Razabil Fortress', roared with noise
As mist from river cleared.

A hill called Tortoise was assailed
Dive bombed by air command;
Artillery o'er mountain, hailed
Great tanks, then fully armed

Cut tidal estuaries, to drive
Tank, straight on top of gun;
These missions as these brave men dive
Make heroes, every one.

For three full days, our tanks aspire
Japs' bunker system, wreck;
Elaborate, this foe not tire,
Set up to save their neck.

Japs tunnelled thirty feet below
This labyrinthine strength;
Taught first lesson we must follow
Our pause was of wrong length.

We needed to reduce the time
Between the tanks' first round;
Tank gunners worked their pattern fine,
Prized earth round bunker's ground.

A high explosive burst inside,
This plan repeat again;
As Infantry reached bunker's side
Midst undergrowth of flame.

King's Own Scottish Borderers saved
By ghost train, misty hazed;
Ngakyedauk Pass, we paved
So gripped a foothill raised.

Supporting troops made home-made craft
As Africans too ply;
Like midget floating fort a raft
In midstream floated by.

The Japanese had grand design
Known 'Operation C';
They planned to split and cut our line
Kill each separately.

Launch blow in Manipur, once there
The Allied Front surprise;
The road to Chittagong laid bare,
Hoped Bengal would uprise.

Three task forces were planned to hunt
As Japanese evolve;
To smash the Allies' Centre Front
And Victory Plan resolve.

This bold articulated plan -
Attack with headlong speed;
The enemy used every man
Quite sure he would succeed.

Without their guns the gunners fought -
To capture ours, arrange;
Resistance fierce and stubborn, halt
And face of Campaign change.

Christison, sensing trouble near
Sent Seven Div. Brigade;
Reserved for later brings up rear
As tanks' deception made.

Where fog lay thick and grey in glen
And pack mules creak and list;
Tornado of eight thousand men
Struck hard with action swift.

Brigade Headquarter's telephone
Had line near river, slashed;
Nor those that reconnoitred, shown
Where ration convoys, clashed.

For refugees had not been seen,
Were, not known being killed;
But, driven by the Japs to screen
As from the North they spilled.

Deep in the valley flared the flames
Where Gurkhas joined with tank;
Then rose a cheer like those in games
Arousing all in camp.

Waist high in mist, the hidden foe
Pierced only outer fringe;
Brought mortars fast, to fire and go
Headquarters to impinge.

The corps Admin Box had one link
In touch with outside world;
Messervy had recourse, to think
With grenades to be hurled.

Prowling, attacking units small
As Box in four hours reach;
Patrols and snipers, gunners, all
Infested flooded creek.

Here, signalmen devised a plan
Their own code they employed;
With local jokes a message ran
Or with French words, decoyed.

With wireless gone they set about
As each event transpired;
These signalmen gave orders out
Imagination fired.

The Japs threw out right flanking force,
Descended on the pass;
Communications cut at source
Continue to harass.

Victorious, march on Delhi
While fires the jungle heat;
Stage one of 'Operation C'
With great joy, think complete.

'The Rose of Tokyo', soft sung,
Told, "Burma's at an end";
But air support was now begun
To trapped troops quickly send.

Mountbatten's promise showed the ways,
Drive Japs from circling lines;
Supplies and rations for ten days
Held near for such bad times.

Major General Snelling gave
First service of the year;
And many more there were to have -
Eliminate all fear.

For combat side was wide awake,
Slim brought out of reserve;
Both Indian Brigades to take
With cool courageous nerve.

Twenty-Sixth and Thirty-Sixth
Divisions, held to bring
In readiness with Festing fix -
Brigaded, everything.

Not time to question Fate's ill quirk
Or place to wring his hands;
Men shape to change, together work,
Pull back from sinking sands.

This medley of eight thousand men
Were some of every kind;
Road builders, sappers, signalmen
With doctors brave, to find.

THE BATTLE OF THE ADMIN BOX

Royal West Yorks and Gurkhas formed
With Twenty-Fifth Dragoons;
As Infantry defence performed
With lorries with platoons

In which the Japanese full slept
Their orders to preserve;
So rigid were these rules so kept
That No Man's Land, conserve.

Fight hand to hand as probe to glean
Through misty light of day;
On moonless night without a beam
Could scarcely find the way.

This truly was a desperate fight
A soldier's battle prove;
All seized a gun together might
Of enemy, to move.

In paddy field of rice, now dried
An area like a cup;
In vain the enemy all tried
Resistance to disrupt.

The Spitfires fought, and Zeros lost -
We unimpeded flew;
And Japanese found to his cost
That we could win anew.

Here dominate a ring of hills -
We could not man them all;
For this was one of many ills,
On few men could we call.

Old's Troop Carrier Command
Brought its defenceless bulk;
Like massive boat that quite unarmed
Has no protected hulk.

Both day and night made presence known
These saviours on high;
And sixty tons was daily thrown
Down hatchway of the sky.

Combined, the 'Op of pilots', win
With different countries' force;
To keep their heavy ships in trim
To steer their wayward course.

Nine hundred sorties now took place -
Three thousand tons were dropped;
Kit, oil and petrol, food replace
As through sharp contours, hopped.

A new concept to build upon
Of each man's single worth;
In sky, on ground, as they fought on
This fresh idea took birth.

High clouds of smoke rose all day long
As new explosions burst;
And wounded operated on
Near spot where they fell first.

Built into tree trunks, hidden well
The green clad snipers aimed;
Or, roped to trees our men to fell
As many victims claimed.

Major Lilwall, D.S.O., manned
The dressing station's hill;
And miracles that quite unplanned
Were wrought for every ill.

Then came a sudden burst of flame
And sixty Japs rushed in;
No mercy showed with fury aim
Alone, by foul means win.

In cold and calculated thought
They slaughtered all round;
The sick, avoiding getting caught
Though wounded, crawled on ground.

Six doctors bullets through the ear
Were killed in coldest blood;
But later, Japs, West Yorks to fear -
Avenged, where rivers flood.

Around the Box the battle raged
As sun fell over range;
In weirdest masks Japs warred and waged -
To animals they change.

Everything they had, men shared
To mending slacks, to shirt;
Or telling thought to those who cared,
Cheered healing spirit's hurt.

The bottom of a slit trench deep
With grey fat rats, to share;
Men found it safest there to sleep
As if they had no care.

Most gallant part the Air Force played
For many wounded saved;
The Hundred and Fourteenth Brigade
Light aircraft, channel paved.

Now role and spirit on each side
Significant, arrange;
Briggs' Fifth Division stubborn hide -
Japs' High Command not change.

Their timetable in ruins lay
Beyond allotted span;
Of seven days when ceased to slay -
Used, rations of each man.

Fresh troops were coming from the North
Who made the Japs deter;
All force their plan had carried forth
But we more violent were.

First battle's phase ordained by Fate
Now opened, neared its end;
Jap recast programme was too late -
Messervy's tanks we send.

Christison's plan, destroy two-fold
Fierce enterprise of foe;
The first, reopen coastal road -
The second final blow.

Sharp spine of range to clear and sweep,
Dispatch Japs by the score;
As pincer movement strong and deep
Grips with its savage claw.

So, Fourteenth Army won these parts
Paved way to Imphal Plain;
Another drama also starts -
The Great West Way of Fame.

These Africans through jungle thread
Five days without a pause;
Sound hunting horn as Japs fast fled
Are vital to our cause.

Counter-offensive British made
On both sides of the range;
At Razabil Fifth Div. portrayed
A massive barrage change.

The strongest citadel of all
The Thirty-Sixth Div., breached;
They caused a six inch gun to fall
And ammunition reached.

In light of the full moon to fire
A concentrated blast;
Assault, that gave all we desire -
Victory, at last.

A special force of bearded men
In March of Forty Four;
Were gathered for invasion, when
A great idea explore.

So, Long Range Penetration grew
With policy most wise;
Involved ten thousand men who flew
In battle dress disguise.

OPERATION THURSDAY

"The guts of enemy to pierce,"
Was Wingate's major aim;
To hit him hard in war so fierce
And make him writhe in pain.

A thousand pack mules fell as well -
They all were dropped at night;
Like plumbing depth of deep dark well
With moon and stars for light.

Intrepid was this special force
Some, Cochran's Circus, named;
So Wingate's Chindits trained on course
That through the world is famed.

Men who mastered both the art
Of gliders' lift and tow;
On Operation Thursday start
To travel to and fro.

Relieve, replace and not withdraw
Began with great dismay;
As 'Piccadilly' showed before
Huge trees in her path lay.

A switch to 'Broadway' was ordained,
"A better place we've found";
Was how this change of place explained
By Cochran on the ground.

This aerial train rushed down the strip
And dust a whirlwind blew;
Bounced, swayed and strained in wind to whip
Cast loose, o'er trees it flew.

Eight thousand feet of mountain heights
Great faith they must renew;
As flying blind without their lights
Surprise tactics were new.

Once penetrated deep must then
Have power to mainstay;
The wounded save by skill to stem
And snatch from where they lay.

Gun, wagon, animal and jeep
On slender towrope ride;
As gliders sail while other sleep -
To stop the war's grim tide.

Then heavy wireless sets they read
As crashes soon occur;
In jungle wounded cry and bleed -
In wrong direction, err.

For control glider forced to land
On Chindwin riverside;
Made others overshoot as spanned
Crash hard as fast they glide.

Frantically they tear, where blown -
Their muscles in great pain;
To extricate where grass is grown
Deceptive on terrain.

The total sum of dead they make
The sum of twenty-three;
As surgeons work to amputate
To set the wounded free.

Four hundred men were safely hoist
Together with much store;
But mechanised equipment foist
To lose for evermore.

As early dawn cast its first beam
The U.S. engineers
Of Nine-Hundredth Field Unit Team
Hand level as day nears.

Then transportation organised
Troop Carrier Command;
Their reinforcements galvanised -
Bring wounded back to land.

Where fifty five Dakotas came
Flew five nights without a hitch;
Six hundred sorties all the same,
Not single one they ditch.

The gliders slipping silent past
Join traffic in the sky;
Nine thousand troops transported fast,
With guns and mules they fly.

In four days columns marched ahead
Down jungle tracks they went;
Their aim to cut the links and tread
Where Japanese were sent.

Wingate built a new stronghold near
As enemy react;
When Fergusson had hacked it clear
Bombed gliders' burned out tract.

Now Brigadier Tom Brodie came
With Chindit Fourth Brigade;
But Wingate's death now left a name
As legend great, he made.

A seal was set upon the 'Man'
Whose plane was lost in storm;
To crash in flames as mountains span
Left battered topi, torn.

Romantic mystic died in prime
His finest exploit cast;
No more a ringing clock to chime
To tell us time has past.

He pattern placed on jungle fight,
Left Lentaigne his command;
This trusted solider on his right
Had made him fully armed.

A Mitchell bomber's charred remains
Holds secret of his grave;
So now we turn to seek these claims
By Chindits true and brave.

Take Fergusson the six foot Scot
With monocle in eye;
Who led on foot to plan and plot
Through undergrowth grown high.

With gradient of one in one
All crawled on hands and knees;
In day dried out by noonday sun
At night in dew, to freeze.

There was no trail they made their track,
With hatchets hacked away;
The Chindit's Oscar's massive back
Held sick in gentle sway.

He was beloved this mascot bull,
To Ledo led his hooves;
For many wounded men to pull
Along these man-made grooves.

THE WAR OF THE CHINDITS

The roar of planes above in mist
Was heard by hungry men;
Who see them dive with fearful risk
Through grey shroud of a glen.

The precious load about to land
Is lifted by a breeze;
Like some malicious hidden hand
Denies, their right to seize.

Obliterating as they must
Their footsteps secret track;
They worked in pairs, swept marks with dust -
At smelling jungle, hack.

A hundred miles is covered each
By hungry weary file;
Then tawny River Chindwin reach -
At edge they camp awhile.

The drone of aircraft humming clear
As throb of engines sound;
And flashing message high appear -
Sacks cascade to the ground.

The Leicesters then a bridgehead built
With boats on gliders towed;
On sandbank loaded to the hilt
No casualty they showed.

A detour marched by this deploy
Gained victory so bold;
At Lonkin detailed to destroy
The Japanese stronghold.

So Aberdeen was fortified
Now Indaw they attack;
By forces grim they were denied
With Brodie both drew back.

From Broadway Calvert struck out West
The railway to assail;
A block 'White City', built with zest
Was scene of much travail.

The savage fighting through the night
Like mediaeval feud;
Showed in the day how grim the plight
Of bodies hacked and hewed.

The Air-Commanders planted load
And high explosives land
On concentrations on the road
Of Japanese, at hand.

To Hopin Valley next they turned
Lentaigne's old stamping place;
Called 'Blackpool', here he now returned
Hope, Japanese replace.

But Japs ferociously defend
As our brave troops attack;
Their efforts here they had to end,
Go through the morass, back.

Wingate gathered all his men
The day before he died;
"One day, all will be proud of them,
Those who were here!" he cried.

This grim campaign so hard and long
With household on their back;
Scrub-typhus, jaundice, that prolong -
Endurance nearly crack.

STILWELL'S ROAD

British, Africans, carry load -
Indians, Gurkhas fight;
Americans built the Ledo Road
In secret laboured might.

While stores of war rolled on and on,
Took tears and sweat and blood;
A two-mile wooden causeway won
Road rose above the flood.

Twelve thousand miles of sea and land
Their great equipment crossed;
In these wild hills of swamp and sand
In red mud, mules were lost.

To liberate North Burma now
And meet with China's Land;
These men who hand turned to the plough
As operation planned,

Were Chinese trained by U.S.A. -
Merrill's Marauders, joined;
'Twas after Frank Merrill they say
This nickname had been coined.

They drove the Japanese before,
Swept deep into the hills;
Caused enemy to worry more,
Add to their many ills.

The highway builders blasted track,
Cut swathe twice wide as road;
So forces cut Japs' rear - distract
As enemy they goad.

Piled, slashed and hauled this varied force -
Men yellow, black and brown
With white, two thousand built a course,
And oil pipeline laid down.

At one time tanks called on for strength
These peasant boys, fast milled;
They held the Japanese at length
As four thousand they killed.

Their hara-kiri method shows
How they were lost and dazed;
The Fourteenth Army parried blows
And gun emplacements razed.

The Eighth Route Army were Chinese
Whose walkers are the best;
Who carry all on pole with ease
Six thousand miles with zest.

The local Kachin tribesmen claimed
Uncanny sense to find;
The Japanese they killed and maimed
As seemed to read their mind.

On Kamaing Stilwell's forces hailed
On Seventeenth of May;
While Nauri Hykit Pass was scaled
By Merrill's men that day.

And when they were cut of by land
The gliders all sailed in;
So Myitkyina fell to hand
As close support all bring.

A siege of foot by foot they fought -
The will of one man, shield;
The inspiration that he taught
With only stick to wield.

The Ledo Road joined hands at last
With Burma Road, its strength;
From Assam to Kumming it passed
A thousand miles in length.

One hundred thousand Japanese
Fought 'Operation U';
They hoped to win the war with ease -
Pierce bayonet, quick through.

So Baldwin, Slim and Scoones conferred
And Imphal Battle planned;
All air supply for Japs, deferred -
Alternatives they scanned.

The Field of Manipur Japs chose
To seize the Imphal base;
And Bengal Assam railway close,
Our planes off 'Hump', to chase.

Commander Slim had choice so fine.
His troops o'er Chindwin fan;
Or fight the Japs on Chindwin line?
He, Imphal Plain did plan.

THE MARCH ON DELHI

On plateau green on borderland
The British formed their base;
They built large depots, dumps to hand -
Two airfields also place.

The gap called Kalewa was doomed
If British held the plain;
Here, heart of Japs' great power, bloomed -
Defend 'till all were slain.

The Lightnings and Mustangs far fly
With R.A.F. employ;
The Oscars and the Dinahs try
In vain these to destroy.

Atrocious weather now was felt
With pre-monsoon was dust;
And after clouds banked in a belt
And storms with rainfall, thrust.

Three Indian Divisions here
At Ukhrul while they wait;
Like jungle Stalingrad not fear
The enemy at gate.

In spite of hardships orders came
From Japanese Command;
Thrust each division, three to name
But, failed, supplies of arm.

On March the Fourteenth orders sent
To Cowan told to go;
And swift and fast he packed and went,
Left Tiddim's burning glow.

Four thousand mules in darkness grope
Up tricky mountain side;
Two thousand vehicles to cope
With animals, they hide.

The Seventeenth Division fought
And many roadblocks laid;
Full under fire they havoc wrought
And Japs to their God, prayed.

The Twenty Third Division lick
The raiders, help our men;
And Gracey with his dog and stick
Withdraws, as orders pen.

The march toward Imphal was grim
Dead only left behind;
And air supplies came flowing in
With help of every kind.

On evening of St Patrick's Day
Japs swift and silent streak;
And from the Somra Hills they pray
Thank Gods to whom they speak.

Puffed up with victory all gazed
And wireless screamed full blast;
The Flag of Rising Sun was raised
On Indian soil at last.

To Kohima a punch was packed
Too many and too soon;
Mountbatten sent the men we lacked -
Arose from darkened room.

His eye was hit by bamboo stake -
In hospital he lay;
But signals came so off did take
The enemy to slay.

At Kohima we concentrate
As reinforce the plain;
For Japanese then infiltrate
But strength was but in vain.

Offensive springboard we had built
Slim's reinforcements fell;
In fighting men armed to the hilt,
A secret all held well.

Machine guns, infantry and tanks
With bullets cannonade;
To Allied Air Force we owe thanks
As victory we made.

First Corps and Fifth Division wait -
Loud salvoes thunder out;
And in the air we then frustrate
With twenty squadrons, rout.

The two to one's group air defence
To Surma Valley base;
Each night they flew to recompense
As tired crews replace.

Communications we destroyed
It was the final blow;
Ten days was up and march employed -
This Japanese could show.

They footed miles so short of food
Appalling methods, vied;
Now rail and river were no good
And many thousands died.

We thirty thousand wounded flew
Without a single loss;
Three hundred planes a day, renew,
Their bounty freely toss.

A graver state at Kohima
With roads cut into town;
And tree, bungalow and bansha
By barrage blasted down.

For fifteen thousand Japs attacked
Against three thousand men;
With few supplies as airstrip lacked
Mountbatten quickly send.

THE STAND AT KOHIMA

To Fourteenth Army quarters, tore
To help the troops in need;
Brings Indian Thirty-Third Corps -
Moves troops in record speed.

To link with Fourth Corps in the plain
Fourth Royal West Kents came;
Whose fighting courage not in vain
Though many of them slain.

British objectives were outlaid -
Both Kohima relieve;
One-Hundred-Sixty-First Brigade
Drive Japs away from siege.

The Allied Air Force gave support
Bombs into gun pits fell;
Their ammunition as they fought
Most welcome in this hell.

The Highlanders of Cameron
Relieved the First Brigade;
Linked hands so they could carry on
As second phase now made.

Supplies were getting very short
For water, pint a day;
They crept in close where Japs near fought
It was the only way.

For two weeks they had no respite
With two hours sleep on end;
Resources for the sick so slight
That very few could mend.

Re-wounded they could only lie
In line of mortar fire;
And Colonel Young saw many die
In situation, dire.

Kungpi village five times changed
In Summerhouse Hills' plight;
So bloody did the fighting range
By Japanese at night.

The rags that hung on shell-shorn trees
Bore witness to a scene;
As spirit shrinks as disbelieves -
Could this be a bad dream?

The Camerons and Worcesters took
Guns, engineers and tanks;
Broke through the blocks and wounded look
To them, to give their thanks.

For fifty days and nights men stayed,
Their backs were to the wall;
Those who survived as hard they prayed
Obeyed strict duty's call.

The Royal Berkshire Regiment
Now marched to save the siege;
From heaven were these soldiers sent -
'Twas too hard to believe?

Our columns scaled ten thousand feet
With loads upon their backs;
By ten to one we Japs defeat
Whilst carried heavy packs.

The Centre Point was at 'Jail Hill',
So frontal assault formed;
For three long days and nights to spill
Men's blood as bunkers stormed.

So ridge at Kohima we took,
At 'Church Knoll' fork Japs out;
For fifty days and nights earth shook
As enemy we rout.

The six hundred square miles of plain
Contain no living Jap;
Thus front at Manipur we gain
So Stopford turned to map.

The Fourteenth Army caught in claws
Imphal-Kohima Road;
At Ukhrul gripped in snapping jaws
Like that that traps a toad.

The terraced dead, whose names now spell
Out valour, hold their own;
These places where men fought and fell
In History go down.

Defensive now the Japs hit back -
We, their Divisions, take;
Our twenty thousand shells fast track
Drop, and resistance break.

The Indian Divisions climb
With mountain guns they fight;
Through misty blanket firing line
In monsoon, out of sight.

On bloody plain Jap solider killed,
"They never will come back";
The Fourteenth Army flag now thrilled
Dead..... fifty thousand Jap.

On August seventeenth, the month
In nineteen forty four;
Took Bishenpur far to the South -
Freed India from the war.

"Jap soldier, man for man we've thrashed
In greatest combat yet;
Next year will have their army smashed
In way they'll not forget."

The battle is the pay off, but
Is also something more;
It is effort after tuning up
And training's slogging chore.

MARCHING SOUTH

To hang on heels of broken foe
Is hard but must be done;
He flies on fast in haste to go
But battle not yet won.

Kimura played into our hand
There was not time enough;
For Japanese to make their stand,
The going was too rough.

We harried the retreating Jap,
Air forces hammered hard;
Grim skeletons in staff cars sat
In convoys burned and charred.

Their fighting will was broken fast
With only rice to eat;
Before their gold-leafed idols cast
Sore bodies, starved and weak.

The suicidal squads brave showed
As pouring rain conspired;
Contest each foot of Tiddim Road
Mined, booby trapped and fired.

The British path by landslides stopped
While bridges swept away;
Torrential rain in fury dropped
As monsoon held its sway.

Entire supplies dropped from above
Brave nurses' march they share;
Raised troops' morale this woman's love
Was shown in tender care.

New bridges sappers built with haste
From cliffside highway carved;
Across the purple jungle faced
By Japs posts now left halved.

The Chocolate Staircase terraced length
Our troops lined with supplies;
Like yellow ribbon of great strength
Lies on the blue hillsides.

Dogra Regiment patrols crossed
Beltang Lui by night;
And tanks loomed out where clouds embossed
Bore headlamps to give light.

Peak Kennedy in front they saw
With stronghold named Fort White;
Below mist blanketed Kabaw
A pestilential sight.

The fortress in the clouds was stormed
Like struggle in a shroud;
Through fog the gunners' pieces formed,
Planes drop supplies through cloud.

Well-sighted bunkers trenched in ground
For Japanese defence;
Were straffed by squadrons and so found
In valley of death hence.

December night at Kalewa
Saw echelons led past;
Across the Chindwin travelled far
Where once retreated fast.

Across long Bailey bridge Slim led
His single army, great;
The feat of Nations' efforts sped
To seal their foes' ill fate.

This was Chindwin's regatta day
Armada of all craft;
Converged to make the water spray
Upon them, fore and aft.

As Fourteenth Army quickly moved
To plain o'er Mandalay;
Support by air again was proved
To show success the way.

Super Fortresses smashed yards, far
In the enemy zone;
One thousand and four hundred are
The miles they flew from home.

Beaufighters fire their cannons flamed
At traffic closing near;
Japs, them 'Whispering Death' nicknamed,
Closed all in silent fear.

North Combat Area Command
Formed Mars Force on that day;
Sent now to train their men on land
Stilwell to U.S.A.

And General Festing took Taungyi
Down railway corridor;
Twelve thousand shells shoot at Pinwe
As monsoon rains down pour.

R.E.M.E. men found a track
Along their axis ran;
Made locomotives as they hack
And salvage all they can.

Ten loaded trucks raced fast downhill
At forty miles per hour;
Tall Festing drove his jeep with skill
As harnessed all this power.

Supplies dropped, U.S. Tenth Air Force
With bombers gave support;
While Mobile Hospital, recourse
Where Chinese British fought.

Three men succeeded Stilwell, set
With Wheeler to command;
Major-General Fuller met
With Sultan close at hand.

So through the Hosi Valley razed,
Made rotting ruined place;
Royal Sussex Regiment raised
Union Jack's fair face.

Large Y Force of Chinese converge
On Salween River, toss;
Four hundred rubber boats emerge
As forty thousand cross.

Where sleet and snow and fog fast whirled
On Himalayan height;
On front the hardest in the world
In shorts and sandals fight.

For months the battle ebbed and flowed
On unreported Front;
Now open Indian Chinese road
As Japanese they hunt.

With unexpected speed Slim's men
Leave stealthy jungle fight;
Adapt themselves from darkest glen
To open country's light.

THE ROAD TO MANDALAY

On Mandalay all force converge
As Campaign's pattern showed;
Behind great river Japs emerge -
For Slim new problems posed.

Lieutenant General Leese was told
To haste and seize Rangoon;
For to secure the Burma Road
Must strike before monsoon.

Mountbatten reinforced and planned
Amphibious fleet required;
And sea-borne landings quickly spanned
As he his men inspired.

Across charred bodies of the dead
And shattered foxholes reach;
Attacking soldiers quickly sped
As shellfire blast and breach.

So Sutton and Christison met
And Lashio contain;
And Akyab and Ramree get
Secured where airfields lain.

Withdrawal of Dakotas meant
Entire offensive slowed;
But Browning increased supplement
To cross where river flowed.

And Japanese now concentrates
By Irrawaddy hides;
But Slim against rear infiltrates
To thrust hard with surprise.

The timber that grew on the bank
Slim's men like shipwrights seem;
The boats they made were seldom sank
But floated fast on stream.

The Royal Navy now had ship
That by the Army built;
Where Bofors and Oerlikon spit
Their cannon up to hilt.

A fake Corps H.Q. chose to use
So Japs massed high with gun;
Slim masked deception of the move
Then blasted as they come.

Now set for battle was the scene
With three Divisions crossed;
Both air and motorised between
So Japanese were lost.

As 'Dagger Div.' surged southward fast
Leese hammered all the way;
Across the golden shrines of past
They fought for Mandalay.

The battle of the plain raged on
Until the tide was turned;
The British and the Indian throng -
Shot, bombed and hacked and burned.

So in the 'City of the Kings'
Like butterfly in Spring;
A white flag fluttered like white wings -
Relinquished everything......

Shut in by bamboos' forest cane
And sixty miles from sea;
The last Campaign in Arakan
Was of necessity.

WAR IN THE CHUANGS

To Ramree Island sailed our craft
Beneath the bombers' shade;
The Indian Corps struck hard and fast
At Chuang bridgehead made.

Mountbatten sent Christison's force
As Japanese gave in;
Left Akyab to change their course -
We vital airfields, win.

The Fourteenth Army rolled ahead
Through snipers' paradise;
The suicidal Japs all bled
Locked in grenades' tight vice.

As prey to flies, mosquito stings
And crocodiles' dread bite;
Poisoned as the scorpion clings
The enemy took flight...

Fierce 'Bunker Busting', no one shirked
We turned the battles' tide;
Outfought outwitted and outworked,
Japs' screaming frenzy died.

The Fifteenth Corps sailed to Rangoon
To take it from the sea;
In haste they raced against monsoon
As storm clouds clustered free.

And air supply is rated high,
Without their 'Wings', their might;
Unfailing in their great supply -
Impossible to fight.

The wounded in the wilderness
Were rescued, kept alive;
We these mercy missions bless
As helped them to survive.

The fighters and the bombers raced
Ahead our foes to blast;
On transport hailing bullets traced
As monsoon broke at last.

On May the second Rangoon fell
As troopships loaded shell;
A sampan held two airmen tell,
"Japs gone, we've lived in Hell."

THE FALL OF RANGOON

Burma was conquered from the North
This never done before;
Mountbatten and his men brought forth
The road to Singapore.

Malaya now we planned to take
The Twelfth Army avenge;
Jap, retribution had to make -
Enacted, swift revenge.

Twenty thousand Japs were killed
And others followed suit;
And so their starving blood was spilled,
Acknowledged, their deep guilt.

Command now of the Japs' Armed Force
Surrender all the way;
To troops and Singapore's concourse
Mountbatten, had, his say......

As hidden Union Jack unfurled
And flown for victory;
This Burma Tale told to the world
In glowing history.

JOURNEY'S END.

WAR POEMS

WINSTON CHURCHILL'S WAR DECLARATION

(Hammersmith Hospital, September 1939)

Even now when I pick up my pen
I shrink from the terrible past;
"At war, what us and who with and when?"
The questions fall thick and fast.

White-aproned, wasp-waisted and willing
I hear the words that boomed out on that day;
Spoke a message both fearful and chilling
As to God we all silently pray.

Nothing was ever the same
For this country we all love so dear;
Not a game today, no, not a game
As the wail of the sirens whine clear.

The beds in the ward hold the frail
The sick and the old who once fought;
"A war to end war", no avail
Echoes in souls overwrought.

As the sun gleamed its pale yellow light
To glitter on glass window panes;
They feared that the end was in sight –
Imagined engulfed in red flames

Which once flamed long ago, now repeat
Full circle – with life almost done;
A new vicious circle complete
What was once in their lives overcome?

Stay strong for these souls, hold steady
For those who faith once brightly burned;
Have the bedpans once more at the ready
As normality slowly returned.

THE MUNICH AGREEMENT

(30 September 1938)

Here, Churchill's words momentous spoke
On first day of The House;
As Munich gave the Czechs no hope
In game of cat and mouse.

"Herr Hitler's force of arms, war's grist
Thus, by this violent token
His language of the mailed fist;
All's over, silent, broken."

"Do not suppose this is the end,
Now, reckoning begins:
There, forty million Germans rend
As beckoning, each sings

And cheers as stamping feet crash out
When Führer's speeches spell
Their golden future's god-like rout -
Predict each country's hell."

"Democracy is real and free
And people questions ask:
Will sacrifice most willingly
If told the strength of task."

WINSTON CHURCHILL

This man, this Churchill, is portrayed
By many writers since:
A man injustice made enraged,
Who caused all fools to wince.

He led in carpet slippers, clad
In zippered boiler suit:
A politician often sad
He, enemies left mute.

A fine and noble cause he fought
Tenaciously, his power
Was uncorrupt: this lesson taught
As served 'His finest hour'.

A message flashed across the line
"Winston is back," it told:
September third of Thirty Nine
We'd leader brave and bold.

To lead them in the task ahead
They, Winston Churchill knew
As person best they chose as head,
With British instinct true.

The dreadful words "We may be licked,"
Drove Winston to this speech:
"It may be true, we may be stripped
Till Victory we reach."

"It may be true that steel and fire
Will rain upon us soon:
Our food supplies in peril dire.
Spend day and night in gloom."

He said, "Blood, tears and toil and sweat
Be offered to us all:
Survival we could only get
If obeyed strict duty's call."

Now, sixty five years old, he scorned,
Not 'Old Age Pension' draw:
But Coalition Party formed
In Cabinet of War.

In politics, his greatest gift
Was magnanimity:
From Victory he would not shift,
Used this word constantly.

Thus spoke Lloyd George a staunch old friend
In speech so full of praise:
"His dauntless courage never end,
He'll fight for better days."

His critics spoke against his name
As France began to fall:
In Paris burning archives flame
As rallied fast, to call:

Monsieur Reynaud in fiercest voice,
"We'll starve the Germans out:
Destroy her towns, she'll have no choice
As we her armies rout."

The R.A.F. three hundred 'planes
Had lost when over France:
Though many Huns shot down in flames
We, could not take the chance

To give the French all 'planes they ask,
Though ten more squadrons give:
And twenty five keep for the task,
So Britain, safe, may live.

His Chief of Staff remained, Ismay -
They both Hindustani spoke:
For secrecy this Code they say
Was used as movements, cloak.

Norway they knew was a mistake.
We sent four thousand men:
A hundred thousand Germans make
Quick victory for them.

While France was crumbling with no hope
Churchill went down 'The Hole':
Here, thought to direct the War - thus spoke
"I'll die first trapped like mole."

The Belgian Army Huns defeat,
Our men not duty shirk:
On May the twenty sixth retreat
Of British from Dunkirk.

French leader he in Paris, see
With great emotion cried
That wounded were the last to free:
On this course must decide.

The scenes amazed those who looked on,
At South East ports they stand:
With spirit still unbroken, come
These brave men of this land.

Leave, where attached by shell and 'plane
Like end of ghastly dream:
These Allied soldiers fast they came
In tired unending stream.

A million men plucked from the fight
As evacuation cease:
Equipment lost in dreadful plight ......
Begin again, for peace.

"We'll fight on beaches and on field
In streets and in the hills:"
Said Churchill, "We will never yield
They'll never break our wills."

So out of wilderness he came,
His candour courage told:
His name became a household word
Where history is told.

As Italy invaded France
In this unlikely hour:
He decided to take only chance
Fight this union that gave power.

This bulldog breed of ruthless might
Spurred every Briton on:
This martial sound called to the fight
Every Briton's son.

"Robots and slaves we'll never be,
For freedom, justice, stand:"
So Mr Churchill's oratory
Was broadcast through the land.

"Civilisation is at stake,
Perverted science, aim:
Herr Hitler's fury tries to break
Our stand against its claim."

Cartoon was shown, by artist, Low
Of soldiers on a cliff:
To flames says, "Very well, alone."
Afar, he shakes a fist.

The U.S.A. had only guns,
For troops they were too old:
So Home Guards' force were given ones
For million dollars sold.

The Vichy Government in rage
Protest to keep their fleet:
In Northern Africa engage
Our Navy meet defeat.

In Berlin Hitler made a speech
"Invasion is most hard;
Most difficult their sea to breach,
They'll fight for every yard."

In that hot summer of July
We won, though great the cost;
'Battle of Britain' fought in sky
And enemy were lost.

So much we owe to men so tough,
So young and brave in fight;
We never can repay enough
Their sacrifice for right.

So Hitler's war lost in the air -
Our policy was wise:
Attack the Nazis' Homeland where
Their bombers of great size

Begin night blitz upon our Isle
By German Lüftwaffe, weak:
From airfields turned as more worthwhile,
And we in deep shelters, sleep.

So Britain her Invasion fears;
She waits and waits in vain
As barges gather danger nears -
Will many more be slain?

Our confidence in Winston held
As 'planes in hundreds, surge;
His marching rhythm of words spelled
To strengthen and to urge.

For seven months morale was high,
Incendiaries fiercely burned
From fifteen hundred fires - we fly
As course of war we turned.

So Hitler's precious time was lost;
Of peace offer was sure;
Rejected fast knew to his cost
Was hard to win this war.

Now, Winston's eyes are brighter, shine
With depths of vision, show
Preoccupied, ahead of time
With resolution, glow.

Rebuking critics, this he claimed,
"This rocking of the boat,
Could be disastrous and ill famed,
Our enemies will gloat."

A special emissary was sent -
Hopkins from U.S.A.:
So, to 10 Downing Street he went
Where Churchill worked each day.

Said "Short and portly man appeared
With beaming rosy face;
Now, know why people he endeared
Of each and every race."

At luncheon they discussed a plan -
The President must see;
All here behind him to a man
But need help desperately.

So Hopkins toured the bombed out docks
And finally went home;
Forged spirit here that interlocks
Both fates by what is shown.

Took Churchill's pills as souvenir,
Were analysed, no good;
But also harmless, thus appear
To do the work they should.

At Chequers, Reynolds also dined
In February, told -
"Antiquity, Winston remind
Of poets, young and old."

His silhouette in doorway thrown,
His figure still like rock;
Cigar at jaunty angle shown
As gothic doorway, block ......

BLACK DOGS OF THE WORLD

(For Lotte)

Nebulous as wraiths that wreath
An unexplored terrain, wrapped
In coils and convolutions
Writhing in an unexpected fashion
To conceal, or reveal?

Shall we discover each other,
Remain involved, convulsed
Volcanic to erupt, when the body
Is corrupt or repulsed?

As the Earth's centre may
One day spill
Split like an apple
To fill the atmosphere
In fragments, inanimate?

FRAGMENT

You went away, the war to fight
And knew the enemy -
Here, ignorance only was my plight
Endured, but silently.

My home and hearth defended well;
Yet, who the enemy?
From happy heaven, into hell
I entered, silently.

Such hope we had, such plans we laid
Were annihilated fast -
The present gone, the future fade;
Now, all was in the past.

My prison cell had door tight closed
So could not venture out -
Strict duty called, strict duty posed
Was borne, in silent shout.

My love, when hope as war did end
Was doomed for evermore -
As coming home, your days to spend
You found a tight shut door.

THE SURVIVOR

Behold, this man, marked with the feel of steel,
His mind's eye blurred; his innocence, which was all he had,
Has gone - destroyed in the fire and fury of a fight
That dragged on interminably;
War is the name of all the horror and fright those years held;
That took his youth, and with it all the giving we call love,
Was lost.

The years between his youth and now, were sterile.
He knows his life was saved, and yet
Was the gain greater than the loss of friends?
He felt betrayed in a way impossible to describe.
The dead were mourned, remembered as heroes,
And they had peace.

It seemed unfair he had not died
In an obvious fashion; that his body's shell
Could walk and talk and go through the motions.
This was not the courage of despair
Only the day and night
Without light, unending;
Faith is the word whose meaning was destroyed,
Together, with his innocence ....

DESERT RAT

(7th Armoured Division)

Laconie you fought in dedicated youth
Withholding gaining nothing for yourself
No monument
But knowledge forged in battle, leaving nothing there
But memories of strength to pillar and subdue
All future torment
That inflames to dust those sad cold charities:
About your head the thunder rolls clear as the gun
Shaking your dream,
Whose rasping file grates upon the mind as sand
That gathers in its golden clasp heaped mound to keep
Accumulate and gleam
Pitiless as the Pyramid: so this age follows
In impersonal wake neglects to thank those
Long forgotten men
But grinds momentous in ever gathering force
For gain and reaps not peace so projects sardonic
On its scattered ken.

THE SNIPER

Yonder, all beyond him dies
As under quiet moon he lies.
A stranger, here, yet brought to pass
Rows of victims, in which tall grass,
Whose wormy stench assigned to gloom
Hold poignancies of ghostly room.

Will it be his to wander free
Away from shade of forest tree;
Hear again the peewit crying,
Lave the pain, decay - the dying
Here does he see the fields of home
Here, find peace where the birds have flown?

"Walk up", quick on the trigger to score,
Labyrinth dark where sun is no more
Shoot behind cover nimble prey
As darts and twists elusive way.
Link flesh with flesh, like fallen leaf,
Or poppy fresh whose dust is grief.

In groping years that follow on,
Most of 'Immortal Band' are gone.
They the few that are still alive
Hold, in their power to survive
A hallowed living whole, who see
'Deserts of Vast Eternity'.

NORMANDY BEACH

Shelter him no longer mine
Tell him goodbye;
Rock gently on the shoreline
Love's lullaby.

Washed clean by the clear seas' flood,
My only dear;
Fear of carnage and of blood
Here, disappear.

Where the lapping waves are free
From war and pain,
In the life-stream of the sea
We'll meet again.

Lacy foam curls round my feet
Weaves garlands gay;
Feeling sun's first early heat
Kissed by spray.

Flimsy flowers frothy white
Form a wreath;
Reflected in golden light
Is no more death ....

THEY TOO
(Reported Missing)

They too, have paid a price for fostering a vision.
Wakeful or dreaming, have done their share of scheming.
Their lives, like yours, were lived out in the searching.

They too, long since became invisible their lives to give;
Now lost, although who knows their once warm breath
May steal alive: caress a prisoner's face?

They too, for Country's love belong, in the silence,
In the song ... to those not left behind ... in the stillness
Of the wind, in the turmoil of the mind.

They too have watched, have waited - heard with bated breath,
Both the silent and the spoken word. - word once adequate,
Now obsolete, now out of date.

They too, echo an heroic scheme of things - express a poetic
Deed to save, to lead: but knew imprisoned doubts
Spread like stiff clay, mixed, that edged a narrow grave.

They too, will join your jostling throng ...
Joyous, they will rise, as on a flight to Paradise
Borne high in glad surprise ... on Angel wings ...

FOR THE VALENTINES

The victory roll, rolled overhead;
At the sky's blue cloak it tore
"Tell us, tell us," the white clouds said,
"Who was it won the war?"

At this, the war scarred Valentines
All mustered to the fore
We've dodged the Huns, and mined the mines;
"But Willie Boy won the war."

The green waves tossed and rolled ahead,
As the Navy piped ashore
"Tell us, tell us," the sea birds said,
"Who was it won the war?"

The gathered Corps, with battle scars
All answered with a roar
"Hear us, hear us," you jolly Tars,
"Boy Willie won the war."

"We know who won the war," they sighed;
"But who will win the peace?"
"Tell us, tell us," the people cried,
"When will the fighting cease?"

47th BRIGADE, BURMA

(For those men who fell by the wayside and were taken prisoner, especially Fusilier Down.)

Sunk in the steamy jungle zone
A humid hut became your home.
Strange insects kept you company
Bird song your only symphony.

Where shadows shield your shaded eye
Beyond the bamboo's bent stalk, spy
In shapeless growth, where first flared hope
Tight twisted shapes of snaking rope.

Despair disallowed all memories pain
Impaled, where impact numbed in vain
The naked nerve - whose shrunken size
Leaves spirit rare as any prize.

To flourish freely as the orchid's
Flaming flower - no more a torrid
Force; but like some cool plant greenly grow
Shooting forth out of the Hell below ......

WAR

When the first shock dispersed,
Then was such pain
As in the beginning
Was child again.

But now, no loud applause,
No laurel wreath
No flowers, no laughter
Only grief.

The body's rigid protest
Can I submit
To the coward soul, cry,
Retaliate, hit.

Against the hollow where
My heart once lay
We made a plan, plotted,
Contrived a way.

Forgot our failures;
Can you forgive
As end the futility
By which we live?

ESCAPE

Hasten all you runners, kick loose dry dust
Past ancient farms where, whispering in thick corn
The crimson poppy strains her head, to thrust
Her paper petals in the dew drenched morn.

Fight abreast the bridge the headlong gale;
Hold your breath, the run's not yet begun.
Keep memories fresh again for fireside tale
Withhold the strength that once a battle won.

The woundings done; leave it and death behind
As leave behind the metre's endless track:
Run to the sun whose yellow light aligned
Go forward now, where once was no way back .....

QUESTION

In the dark time will there be singing,
Will the hibiscus flame its flower
Will the dragonflies still be winging
Will oppressors relinquish their power?

Will the cat and mouse game continue
Will the diving dolphin share
His secluded rendezvous,
With the submarines feuding there?

Nimrods dart down at day's dawning
To the orange enemies' cost;
Shackletons send enemy warning
Nobody won, and nobody lost.

THE PROMISE

You promised to pick apples with me,
But you did not come
You promised to telephone;
But the phone was silent.

You promised to come blackberrying;
But I went alone
You promised with your voice
But your heart was silent.

Only my cat kept her word
And appeared silently
At my door
True to habit
To welcome me ....

KATYN, 1940

Will such stonemason so incline,
Remove sad symbol set on shrine -
Grey obelisk of granite firm -
As flagged and flanked, fixed truth intern?

Equivalent to 'crown of thorn',
Barbed to pierce like devil's horn -
Chaplet so fierce, fresh blood is shed,
As suffused those beholding head

Of suffering Christ, crucified;
Now know for sure, that none have died
In vain - so triple tears we wept
For joy, for rage, for grief so kept

At bay those callous men who lost
'Gainst tangible and tragic cost -
(Which stands, Fate's witness to the glade)
Poles murdered lie, in forests shade.

WAR SONGS

Tipperary, a legendary song
"A long way," yes, "a long way to go";
They sung as they marched along
Quick march, quick march, in a row.

"The White Cliffs of Dover,"
Remember Vera Lynn?
That song she sung moreover
By Jove that girl could sing!

And sweet Laguna Lily,
Marlene's song, to troops;
Both sides sung themselves silly
As she jumped them through her hoops.

Their troubles put in a kitbag,
They packed up with a smile;
Yes, war songs cheered up every lad
Helped slog each weary mile.

ABSOLUTE

Infinitesimal as grains
Of mustard seeds:
Whose Palestinian greatness
All else exceeds;
On whom sly gnawing beetle
Wreaks, to enmesh
As suffocating fumes inhale
Sulphuric hid, streaming eye
Swelled blind behind
The blistered lid .....

The strange fruit reveals a powdered form
Pungent compound white, brown, black
No matter, torn
Yields unguent soothed
To plaster in smooth paste
The slack pierced flesh
Blown up to giant size;
Poisoned as disaster spreads
Like minute toadstools root and cup,
Their night grown heads .....

THE SEA SHALL NOT HAVE THEM

The cruel sea, whose crucial wave,
Crested white, seeks out the brave.
As the wind screams and the spray
Showers white - while clouds of grey
Clustering - to mass and hide
Huddled figures crouched inside
Their frail craft; and the last signal, weak
Maydayed its despairing bleep ....
Far away, the plotters planned
In blue and green the distance spanned.
And nature, treacherous to the end
Gathers force as if to spend

Her energy to concentrate
And that small speck, obliterate ......

THE DIARY

(Anne Frank)

If roses had been in bloom
They'd have drooped their heads in shame;
To see her dragged from the room,
A number, no longer a name.

Words in her diary are brave,
Braver than she herself, knew;
One day the whole world will have
Her testimony, fearless and true.

Imagine a child of your own,
One you cherished, loved to the full;
Your wish, but to see her grown .....
To you, always beautiful.

I had a grim nightmare last night
A man in a garden of rose,
Whipped, as he laughed at my plight,
In rags, without any clothes.

Lucky, I woke - looked around
Covers were all on the floor;
And I was home safe and sound,
Secure, with my own front door.

As the horror slowly vanished
And the band round my heart undone;
I knew Anne could never be banished
She had fought her fight, and won.

Few of this last generation
Left, have this statement to say
"Hold her in veneration,
Go down on both knees and pray

This will never happen to you,
This unspeakable sorrow
For the children of families true,
Never, their victims ..... tomorrow."

THE TANKS

Special breed of men, they manned,
Over No Man's Land, they spanned;
Tumble in sand pit, grumble and roar,
Turn to dust on desert shore.

Lumber like clumsy dinosaur,
Streak ahead, like meteor;
Tumble on gun pit, rumble and roar,
Rust and rot on foreign shore.

Mighty strength that turned the wheel,
Mighty weapon of iron and steel;
Tumble and wrestle, stumble and roar,
Stay warm in our hearts for evermore,

Like fleeting clouds, ghostly and grey
Reveal the sun's metallic ray.

BATTLE OF BRITAIN

He concedes bone - tissue
Sinew, picked thus, bare;
Filled with grace,
His path minutely patterned
To pace with measured tread,
And rhythmic line, to thread.

He precedes skeletal
Veined - new imaged
To magnetise a rainbow
Win a chariot
Through cloud; unknowing
Cling upon Heaven's hem .....

DAWN RAID

Singing raindrops' silver tongue
Weeps upon the hill's green bed;
From their silken shoulders, hung,
Held by rainbow's azure thread

Angels flit their cobwebbed wing
Glory flutters over town;
Wraps your shining form within
Milky, opaled, satin gown.

Stitched with fine seam, carefully
Threaded tight, the purple air
Spins the gold embroidery
Of Sun's bright head, woven where

Cold Northern wind can gnash no more
No night's black shade, no thorn
As yellow sunlight shines before
The ruby eye of Dawn.

SONS

Young hero brave
You were sent shatter'd
To an early grave
Mourned your splatter'd
Blood shed brains spread
For an ideal: not in vain
For once again
A second tried
But he too died
By travesty of fate
An identical wake:
Coincidence
Or providence?
A third discredited
Of a future merited
With distinction, now dead
Adds to the cost
That does not bear the count:
To the mother the account
Is paid – not ever lost.

TRUTH

The Devil laughed, "I'm more than a name,
I've said all I have to say;
I'll show you pictures in fire and flame
Then see if it helps to pray."

"You've tortured the Jews, and committed crimes
That made even me incomplete;
You exceeded in evil, defying all times
That you followed each other like sheep."

"Here is the record, - it flickers and flows
In brilliant coloured angles;
Where the orange and red of the flames really glows,
And the dead lie like melted candles."

"This could not have happened to Uncle Joe,
Or the man who delivers the bread
Or the girl in the wine shop whose skin has a glow;
Not their blood that runs, streaming red?"

"Go on, defy me - you dare not deny me;
This witness the truth testify
Switch off, if you dare - see if I care
I've already seen all of you die .... "

DUNKIRK

I bake a cake
And sit remembering
How you came to tea and said,
"I say, this cake is good"
And how your hand, trembling,
Spilled your tea:
And you apologised.

I remember new tiny lines
That networked round your eyes,
And the unspoken lies
We told each other.
"Oh yes, I'm fine, no sweat,
How's the nursing,
Killed anyone yet?"

And we both laughed,
Confused, a bit in love:
But after promising the next dance
He went to France
And died,
And how I cried and cried
Remembering,

It was Dunkirk, that year,
And every year that day
I shed another tear.

WAR WIDOW

Could you, perhaps
Be prepared
To share, briefly
Your time, with me.
Pause from prettifying
Your home
To talk with me,
Spontaneously?

I know your profusion
Of petunias,
Your glory of
Hydrangeas;
And your baskets - know
Of urns and plants, that
Need your urgent
Attention.

The dog has to be walked,
Friends and relatives
Talked to; the telephone
Answered -
I know all these chores
Take time;
And time is sometimes
Limited -

But while you water
And tender, make order;
I have only my
Tears -
And my aloneness -
Secretly flowering
While I nurture inexpressible words -

MEMORY

(War Bride)

Faint touch of lips that lay
Quiescent:
Faint scent of orange blossom drifts
Poignant
In the humid dark
Light brushing the quivering branch
Stays my path: she has gone
Drifting quietly
As the scented blossom
Before the sun.

REMEMBRANCE DAY

Remember gardens full of flowers,
Remove the gravestone head;
Roll back the years, the days, the hours,
Raise up, the honoured dead.

Remember blood red ruby sun;
Opaque the pearl white moon,
Where sundial's move, as minutes run
Each groove, a glimpse of gloom.

Remember, oh, remember, heart;
Forgetfulness is grief
Foreshadowed, memories shape the dark,
As share, the poppied wreath ......

THE BOMB

Knowledge slow dawning
Of three minute warning –

The notion
Explosion –

What shall be doing
Shall be wooing –

Or crying?
Perhaps dying –

Already
Unsteady –

Imagination falters
As living it alters –

Each moment a last
As hope is held fast –

By splitting the atom
From top to bottom –

Souls are divided
Some are derided –

And others exalted
As pray to be altered –

Some quietly asleep
Too tired to weep –

Wake up to new world –
Unwittingly hurled.

CHINESE GIRL

Where giant pandas print and salamanders sleep on the golden shore
And thrushes sing o'er mountain; was she born daughter
Of the river, where paddy fish and alligators sink and water
Covers them to threaten her no more.
All charm and infinite mystery of the East
Are captured here: no coral island in a tropic sea
Can match her lips like luscious sweetness of the mulberry,
On whose bright fruit the silkworms freely feast;
Or purplish black deep dyed her hair compare.
The strange subdued expression on her face retained as fellow
Ancestors now symbolized – who bound by the Yellow
Sea and seas of South and East – though air
And road and rail now unify their land
Of barren tundra, deserts, islands – are here found
Amongst fauna of diversity enshrined upon a ground
Where giant pandas print and salamanders sleep on the golden sand.

DO NOT CONSORT WITH DEATH

(For Mussolini)

The fiendish plot, played out as he wrote
Of a vicious magician, black masked in a cloak:
To disguise a naked and cruel face;
In subtle satire on the human race.

Gaily they danced as they followed like sheep,
As nerves were twanged tautly with music so sweet:
"Point boy," he sneered, "Point your tongue longer";
Abused, the weak will give way to the stronger.

A soldier stiffened and firmly refused
He stared; he saluted, as caught and confused:
Repelled and repulsed they could not compete;
They applauded, they clapped, they stamped their feet.

His critics were first to fly in defence
Whose side was he on, did he sit on the fence?
Like Judas he kissed his pitiful prey;
In horror, death's hand thus dealt, did betray.

PORT DE MOULIN

(Sark)

Holed, black gaped as teeth
In giant's mouth
With glimpse of rosy gums;
Menaced, cruel as amphitheatre
In great Roman days
When slaves
With childish screams
Tender, light as air
Dived down.

There, white limbs flashed
As gaping jaws
Licked with wet tongue:
Lapped the thick sinews
That glistened
On the bright bleached floor.

Now, red tinged pools float,
Soak
Remaking where the bed
Smooth sanded
Awaits renewal –
As when from foreign shore
Brown clad,
Busy like beaver humped to heave
And strain
Quarry a massive load.

Industrious, intent
St Magloire unfolds his flag of truce
Content,
Illustrious, for ever.

DERRIBLE BAY

(Sark)

The shifting sand invites,
Pushed it piles like cinnamon's
Gritty grains whose soothed syrup
Coats white, or brown when simmered…
And sweet, soaks in spongy depths
To make a fair feast.

Dazzled my eyes drink in
As greedy child devours a cake
Fragrant, fresh baked;
To scoop with silver spoon…
Crumple inlets, caves,
The plate blue ringed clear shining.

Here the sea urchin clings
Sucked tight as lumps
Of treacly quince glued firm
Adhere, smooth as the velvet tongue
Of orchid poked in sandy soil
Lush embedded.

Satiated,
I lie in peace
In a small piece
Of heaven
Nature
Has created.

THE ISTHMUS

(Sark)

Enrapt we contemplate;
Capped, the shell sheer solid
Rising to top, grave
As avid traveller dips thirsty lips
Round beaded rim's iced edge
Whose tears drop like nectar

Ease aching brow which soaks
Drip as dampness breaks
In droplets, slow oozed
To land on dried lips;
Saturated they leak their salt
Flip the taste and touch

Taken over by edged tongue
Tied into rough curl
To roll and savour in its tip.
We gaze on spun gossamer
Captured into thick green plate
Which spreads in graceful pleats

And ripples to fan swirl and undulate
Drape the senses
Which swim, speculate, yearn;
We learn each passing year
The sea unfolds afresh
To give the heart repose, and the spirit rest.

SEA SONG
(Malta)

Why is it when I lie upon the shore bemused, transported to another land,
I hear far clearer sound than does assail the ear in every day;
Sweet music as of seashell made: so high and fierce
To pierce the air; culled from the conch whose clarion call
Rings on beguiling the spirit?
Now, not for me the world of men; aloof I join the world of maidens –
Fish tailed, long haired in streaming seaweed swim as
Dressed in silver netted scales
They sing droll songs of love and happiness. I need no house,
Caves are my home, caverns of stalactite whose pillars
Drip diamonds, and emeralds and pearls.
Dazzled I dive; translucent depths take on new light;
Fair forms float past, on fish's backs they ride
Unhurried, in graceful haste:
Not harried as the ground is plentiful with red rock pools
Lapped o'er with waves. This joyous trance to hold
I dance, held in the grasp of Merman King
Whose Neptuned face gleams white and gold;
While jewelled fingers webbed as swan, glow greenish blue
To clasp my hand.
With dewy tear wistful, wan, his troth does pledge
And we are wed. He guides me to a bed pearled perfect
As oyster shell in which, unsullied, sealed with precious prize
We lie secure; fresh couched bound light with strands
Of fronded ferns that float and feather
Round my aching form.
Then in a boat of mussels made, we ride rough shod
Drawn by a merman grey as silver knight in armour clad.
My tears of salt seep; must I awake
Return to weeping waves, grey, cold as ice
Where seabird grieves for saint of yesterday
The young Cecilia?

BIRTH

Strident noises cease…
Violent voices that impound, assault
The senses, pause in abeyance.
Only now can we savour peace embalmed
Like soft ploy of silken web
Woven lush enclosing a million
Infinitesimal seeds shed for future birth;
Suspend where host
Lies quiet aground
To await impatient, for fruition.
These slight lessons Nature tells…
Listen to a million immortal sounds
That intones as sweet bells
That chime the summer air, lie latent,
Linger light… only then,
Caught in suspension unaware, can we
Employ this Earth's existence:
Unbroken at the peak of our endeavour
Capture whole the spirit's
Enlightenment. On this point
Of time, past, present
And future speak; we balance tense, precarious
As on a tightrope raised
So faint outline is poised
Upon the razored edge.

THE LONDON BLITZ

Now – the island does not even boast regret,
As you let
Your thoughts range back to sloping banks, certain rills
From the hills
Intersect – and give a name to, else they make
Quiet lake.

Back there, green and fresh, the pastures where the sheep,
Half asleep
Crop their fill, and solitude is absolute –
Just the lute
With which note the lark transcends the cloudless blue,
Clear and true.

On this, the site of a London great and gay,
(So they say)
This our country's very capital, your home
Years alone –
Hold your court in, gathered meetings yielding more,
Peace or war.

Oh heart, memory that freezes, slowly burns!
Life returns –
For whole centuries of folly, noise and sin
Shut them in,
With our failures and our glories rest;
Love is best!

OPERATION TORCH

(Rock of Gibraltar)

Amongst green leaves, and out of sight
A tame gorilla sat –
His head was bent, he sought the light
A jigsaw on his lap.
(I looked once more, he did not move
As concentrated hard) –
It seemed that nothing more did love
Than solving Life's Charade.

The more I thought the more it seemed
The strangest thing to see –
Whoever once before had dreamed;
Solve jigsaw in a tree?
But this old chimp was most unreal
In lonely Majesty –
He seldom came, unless to steal;
Down from his mighty tree.

Why should he roam upon the ground
When all was free above –
Where fruit and grains and nuts abound,
But where, oh where, was love?
Young female monkey skittered round,
With bright beseeching eyes –
But bored with her he looked around;
A sleeping dragon spied.

A magic beast, all flame and fire
That came alive at night –
Could jigsaw puzzle light inspire
And come alive tonight?
Could dragon be the missing clue,
Was this the missing name?
He flung his mighty arms, and flew
Into the fiery flame –

The dragon magically all wrapted
This flying, furry frame –
Then, I awoke at last enrapted
By life's enchanting game.
Life's pieces, that enjoined, will make
A picture fair to see –
Are held aloft, one's dreams to shake
By a gorilla in a tree.

THE HEALING HOP

She drank too much, so off she went
A herbalist to find:
He gave her hops from fields in Kent
To help her soothe her mind.

She stuffed them in a pillowcase,
Went hopefully to bed:
Prayed that her heart would cease to race
But slowly beat, instead.

She dreamed a strange and childhood dream,
Of hop-picking again:
Where rabbits dashed with frightened scream
In agony of pain.

But then all changed, the sky was blue,
The golden sun was hot:
The morning came, refreshed anew
Thanks to the healing hop.

So, exorcised of woe and pain,
A moral can believe:
From down the pub can now refrain –
Dried out thus – hops, relieve.

PATRIOTISM

"And did those feet in ancient times?"
His face shines;
"Walk upon England's mountains green?"
Scrubbed clean,
He believes, or half believes the hymn,
It belongs to schools
Discipline and rules.
Older, he will be told to fight -
Not, is it right -
But their right he should die,
Or need cry
Havoc to supposéd enemies;
His mortality
And theirs intermingled,
Jingled.
Nicht de Ruhm,
The rhyme
Supposéd by those others,
Not that men are brothers,
But that country indeterminate,
Should now or late
Determine his fate.

A LEGEND

(H.M.S. Victory)

The painted ships were torn and wrecked
Before the sun went down:
And the Victory led with her flag bedecked
Like a Jewel in a crown.

Though the winds were light and unwelcome gales
Seem to threaten with angry clout
As reefs were shaken out of sails
And the studding sail booms, rigged out.

With hammocks lashed up and stowed on high
Or screened to shield from aim:
And the cockpit prepared where the wounded would lie:
All was ready for Deaths' grim game.

And Nelson prayed and bowed his head,
Left the deck before the start:
In his private diary can now be read
The words most dear to his heart.

Four stars shone brightly upon his breast,
"In honour were gained and in honour shall rest":
On his knees on the quarterdeck he fell
Leaving behind a Legend to spell.

And they took him below and laid him to rest
And examined the bullet that severed his chest:
They said, "He has served his country well
Leaving behind a Legend, to tell."

In duty, valour and facing hell,
With his victories they saw,
A Legend to leave behind as well
Of Master in the art of war.

ALL QUIET ON THE WESTERN FRONT

The Priory bell its message rang -
On a lilac tree's bough, a blackbird sang -
At worded print, stare silently,
Read awful message for all to see.
How link their glorious hopeful sound
Contemplate the gushing wound
The mangled flesh, the fearful stench?
What mind on earth envisage trench
Sandbagged and safe for man and beast
Where rats enjoy a Devil's feast?

For time has telescoped the scene -
Picassoed poppies, red and green
Splash on a canvas, mark each place
Where Judas kissed in last embrace.
The rich brown soil, fertile and fed
By millions of these silent dead.
While all around, the phantom light
Gleams on their crosses sculptured white.
And tiny larks' fresh voices sing
To butterflies on rainbowed wing.

POEM TREE

(For Rupert Brooke)

I dreamed of Poem Tree that grew
Purple fruit like passion's flood
Blossomed ripe as so mysteriously drew
Not Earth's sap: but drops of blood.

I dreamed my Tree took flight and fell
To root again in ancient place,
Where flowers weave a magic spell
For those who plead for Heaven's Face.

I dreamed the fruit and then the flower
Changed to hemlock in which glade,
Black witches brew within the hour:
Where harvest moon shows dead night shade.

I dreamed an earthquake split the land
My Tree was blown across the sea,
There, on an isle of golden sand:
Sweet fruit and flower give back to me.

Oh, happy dream to end in joy
Heaven to Hell then back again,
Such ease my dream loved so enjoy
As only I traverse with pain.

I dreamed once more, and then once more
And every dream contained my Tree,
For here my soul, no longer poor:
Now flourished free in ecstasy.

Another host my Tree concealed
Within a hive of honeycomb,
Such nectar ne'er in life revealed:
Dripped amber dark within its womb.

One time bright birds alighted high
To hide their feathered heads in peace,
And once white cloud of butterfly:
Their flight in endless blue, to cease.

With every dream I gathered strength
To wake each dawn so crystal clear,
To pray, let vision grow in length:
Thus safeguard me from sin and fear.

Last night my Tree spoke soft and low
A melody of silver tongues,
Its leaves, a motion made to show:
Abandonment for all our wrongs.

Oh, precious Tree that sings of hope
Tonight a crimson cloak could wear
Impatient, I in darkness grope:
From daylight cruel and harsh, to bear;

As night owls fix sagacious eye
And myriad moths search out a beam,
Where bats alight on rafters high:
So do my senses in my dream

Soar with unerring aim to where
Proud in primeval glory stands,
To spread its branching fingers fair:
And stretch, to touch, with healing hands.

HEROES

(November 11th, Remembrance Day)

The artist says,
Now, we live in a monstrous Age -
Not in flowers -

But they, they
Feed the Spirit
Of a future Time,
Through their example -
And their
Sacrifice -

They conquered the hobgoblins,
And the dervishes,
The nightmare monsters -

Overcame them all,
(These aged ones)
In Victory.

Those marching feet
Echo like the beat of heart
Or wave,
Continuous, down each
Age -
Faces, bland,
Like gentle babies;
The only difference
Is in the line of hand,
Of wrinkle,
Vein -

Every skein
Tells a story -
Frail breastbones
Are weighted, borne down
With ribboned
Medals
Proudly worn;
Modestly produced
For mothballed suits .....

Afterwards,
On this great Day,
Bands play
'*Abide with Me -*
Abide.'

They sit quietly,
Not speaking,
As the commentator
Makes a sensible
Summing up - Amen:

Melting back into the past,
There is nothing new
For them,
Who in peace and war
Have drunk deeply
From grief's cup -

They span so many years,
Some are over ninety;
But this holds
No fears -

There is no sign of
Senility
In the sagging chin
Line,
The tear that gleams
Under the lid;
In the bagging trouser
Seam -
Gently curving
As the gnarled oak
Bends its boughs
Under the storms .....

THE RED POPPY

A myriad hosts of Heaven will not recompense
For their lost youth
Unknown, heroic overcome; had you died
By whining bullet
Spattering your brain, or been propped mummified
Remote - a lost cause -
Swaddled, left, wrapped as some nameless child
Relinquished; and
Had they lived long as sunflower open to the light
Contains its seed,
They would not begrudge a coin for replica
Of scarlet flower,
One worn on suit to adorn a button-hole; they who had
Borne a million such
Dancing their crimson score in far
Cornfields' rain and sun.

OLD CONTEMPTIBLES

Time does not heed,
It seems unreal -
That you can read
What time reveal -

Cross upon cross,
Sweet flowers bloom -
Tell of our loss
Will you know soon -

Why they had died
With so few years -
Why you now cried
Shed bitter tears -

Remember them,
And place your wreath -
On Heaven's hem
Where no more grief -

Time will reveal
And you'll not need -
(Where all is real)
Your heart to bleed?

WAR SONNET

(For the Tommies)

Behind my sleeping lids
I see them slow march on:
Sleep unbidden bids -
Oblivious, the lark's song
Sings, safe hidden overhead:
Tears fall unchecked, unsaid
Tribute to the long dead,
And we are forever wed
To their forbidden fears, as spurn
To dissemble all these silent years.
Man will erstwhile yearn
For pity, in the vale of unwept tears.
Silent, they tread across times space
Forever set apart from human race.

FEET OF GOLD

Sonnet for Wilfred Owen – War Poet
Killed in action in France, 1917

He heard as in a dream, the guns nearer nearer –
Hastened to leave his trench
Succoured his men remembering dearer dearer
He death defied to wrench.
Draw away and flee, for in that futile fleeing
He knew that he would tread
Towards the guns clearer clearer – all unseeing
Enjoin the newly dead.
Propelled on childhood's golden feet he marched along;
Light of the yellow sun
Lit up a pathway live with linnet's liquid song –
Forever young – become.
War's pity down the years echoes man's latent fears –
War's terror, toil and tears.

BRAINWASHING

(Czech Pavilion, Expo 70)

Everyman derided ...... did you say
The family of man and really mean
Just that, as bad joke, to slay,
Slit; crack open, split a seam

On this Sunday of Progress and Harmony of Man:
Amid the claptrap of words sent to workers,
Prison wardens, washers-up - even the dustman
And flophouse attendant - none for the shirkers.

Electronic sound of psychedelic light
Multi-screen projected, on five screens?
Man moves in blackened tunnel of night
As from womb to womb, maternal screams

And national sounds remembered:
Past Sergeant Pepper in a glass lined tent -
Masai tribesmen - bowler hat assembled
Deserts, typhoons, glaciers - went

To where Czech sinks choked in mindless mire
By those whose doubt, hand in hand with greed
Links with self-abasement; their cries, dire
Greater than life itself, express their need.

They the truth tried
And valued the old way of loyalty
Brother unto brother ratified - and so died,
Ejected in wordless motion, to Eternity.

Then man emerging, sobs himself awake
As from a nightmare grim - feels his heart break.

TIN MAN

His sad clown's face, cocooned in tin
Like aluminium
Foil to wrap cool chocolate in
Like pallid moon or sun.

His meek soul quivers in its mould;
His quaking voice thin creaks;
He lets his drooping lid unfold
Lest eye, saltwater, leaks.

A colour bar alas is found;
Black wars with white and yellow.
Laws that harass, apartheid bound,
Fight shy at silver fellow.

Facts face, as fantasy gives birth
Here, deep dyed as the dawn,
Pink flushing mushroom beds in earth
And Atom Bomb is born.

No mystery for scholar, mild
Film, peace museum, seen
Of innocent and lovely child
Whose great eyes haunt my dream.

The curious queues await their turn
Grey, gruesome relics, see
Dark scars not only bodies burn:
Make souls in purgatory.

The Tin Man grins his dismal grin;
"At least my scars not show
When through the years, the Bell may ring
Time hides his head, held low."

WAR PHOTOGRAPHER

(Life Magazine)

He stands, grave silhouette, hatless against the sky
Stark as slanted scarecrow that surveys
With sightless eye the vast horizon of his bare terrain
Mown down in trice, laid waste.

Time's fickle scythed blade beheads, mutilates
Where crimson flecks the gold as blossoms wait
With lissom grace, sigh, in the soft South wind,
Vital vibrating colour.

Slashed, they are embedded ... ears blocked, he moves
Missioned in second, locked angled acute to seize
The message; communicate grief, which does through pain
This Age, annihilate.

THE LETTER

Infallible stoic
You keep the soul alive:
Spell out a life ahead
Though metallic grows the way
To opaque ponderous strife.
So you alienate
The cancerous, crushing chrysalis
With captive, delicate
And magical words form a Thesis.
Wisest of men you divulge
To those whose small equipage
Slowly dies as the quiet dust
Preserves their conscience
From ..... the telling lies.

I.R.A.

War was once fought with weapon made
Of steel -
The visored knight who drew his sword
In haste -
Whose chivalry at stake would make
Him reel -
Jousting with death, to join the war
Of waste -
Is one of many though the passage of
The years
Has seen all kinds of force that man inflicted,
Rends -
The change is only in the way -
The fears
Remain - today the hooded mask
Lends
To mark the mind - which overwhelmed
Retreats
Into itself - before the truth -
Defeats ....

CORNELIA

(Escape)

There is no inspiration, no aspiring
For Cornelia, her spirit dying
From this alienation of her loves:
So gentle hands, protected once by gloves
Fur-clad lest cold causes stiffened joints to jar
Upon her violin's supple string, strike far
Discordant note shriek in one long silent scream.
What instrument console her, rout her ruptured dream,
Where vapid vacuum is displaced by void; hurled
Black holed, to toil and spin in now distorted world?
Fraught empty arms fashioned to cradle, curve, cup use
With loving care grope in useless gestures: lose
Direction serving the body's rigid stance
To parody her cruel captor's dance.

FALKLAND SAILOR

The pull and pluck of the rushing tide,
The creep of the curling foam;
Oh sea, safe in thy bosom hide
This sailor, far from home.

Fierce flames their fleeting fires, seek
The decks once white and clear;
To lick, consume with cruel heat
His ship, once held so dear.

Black as soot, the billowed smoke
Puffs thick in choking clouds;
Its lethal fumes, like Hell, evoke
Dark shadowed, ghostly shrouds.

Brave and fair, he'll not grow old,
The Spirit of the Sea
Cradles his form to ever enfold
His spirit of chivalry.

THE BARRIER

(Equador)

He leered with a cynical grin,
"Take it away," he said,
"For without the Form filled in
You cannot bury your dead."

"Weep, and continue to forage
For your child drowned in the deep,
Put her in cold storage
For only there will she keep."

Struggle with mud, you Mothers,
Struggle without basic need:
Appeal in vain to your Brothers
In a world mainly governed by greed.

Hold on to your Faith to avenge
In your stilted shanty town
Where not only the vultures scavenge ...
Suffer Life where the Gods also frown.

AERIEL 5

Now, strange and savage the Universe seems;
No longer an object for poets and dreams
Paradisimo lost? Black holes floating past
Suck and swallow the elements, heavy cast.

Twice over they weigh, the battles begin
Gravity fights - first the neutrons all win.
Where do they come from, these greater than lead;
Is there a reckoning for millions of dead?

"Love's always an energy," mystics say.
Is the Universe friendly, must we pray
If God's love is power then dance with delight
With doubts all dissolved in expanse of light?

Strange rapid bursters, ten seconds a time,
Bursting their X-rays - momentum define;
As the black hole disgorges their energies mass
A billion times stronger, where neutrons amass.

So matter piles on - magnetic field draws
Under a canopy - is cast by the laws
Of mind over matter when the roof then caves in
And radiation rained, on the star, held within?

TOSS A COIN INTO A FOUNTAIN

(War Poets Remembered)

This constant fellow, pain, has met his match - for years, I wooed him,
Courted, leagued with him, sought his favour, so that he would plague
Me less; limit his insistence, stop creeping up on me, untoward,
When I believed him sleeping ......

Vanquished, my limbs, somewhat frail, gained momentum as they flee
their Jailer .....

He is forgotten. I cannot imagine him as his image blurs.
Lighter, the day is busy with constant movement.
I note my brighter eye in the mirror, the smoother brow, the upward
Tilt of lips ....

But, what of the other pains where much blood has clogged?
Here, in a heathen sacrifice of minute lives,
Which together pour their spirit, when jabbed and killed,
And terror's first constriction stabbed -
Limp headed in the hand of giants, tremble in twitching agonies ...

Innocent rodent of field and hedge,
Slowly uncoil, with puckered forehead;
All with incurable sores,
Some lame, some blind, clutched in death's jaws still warm;
But very dead;
No longer pluck with tiny claws their downy nests,
But with sharp teeth gnaw their captors.
Crimson, the slaughter stains the cage ......

Not peaceably for them the meadow in the rain -
Exceeding small, they lay down their tiny lives, as life's sweetness vanishes;
Labelled with mechanical callousness,
By man the Victor, the eyes of ice - hands that hold the hardness of
indifference.

Now, I have a greater pain,
More piercing sharp,
In
MY HEART ......

RUDOLPH HESS

Does the punishment fit the crime
Enmeshing tight in web of time;
Do the scales of justice weigh
Impartial, through each second, grey?

Should a law once fair and just
Continue, cruel, to mete and thrust;
Once, when blood was hot and strong
Have we all avoided wrong?

Surely, Time, the Healer, should
Shame past wrongs, make way for good:
Or the jailer and the jailed
In mercy, pity, peace, have failed?

COMPANY

An old solitary lady sat in her flat,
She put on her coat, her scarf and her hat;
She took up her bag, her stick and her gloves
A little old woman nobody loves.

She gathered her ghosts to take on her walk,
She laughed as she listened and joined in their talk;
"She's barmy," they murmured, the couples so young,
"There's nobody there," ... words trip off her tongue.

She smiles as she skips with a hop and a dance,
Her dim eyes a sparkle, her bonnet askance;
"Take my arm, dear," she pleads to her spouse at her side,
"The world is so lovely, the horizon so wide."

"No, the bombs have all gone, peace reigns, this we sought,
Although with your lives this treasure was bought;
Don't go, please wait till we're safe in our home
Then I'll sit with you, silent, until next time we roam."

HOSTAGE

Swift, the horror that confuses
On the sharp outlined face:
Kind, the failing light defuses
This unfamiliar place.

Purple, the barrier
Curtailing recognition;
Death, behold the carrier
There is annihilation

Where the conquerors remain
Fed, fat as the fresh maggots
That devour the flesh, and pain
Beats where the fire-fed faggots

Flame red ... frugal, the cool West
The vast plain, the placid lake;
Impossible to molest
As there is no more to take.

GULF CRISIS

(Panel)

The old General sits on the panel,
His eyes are wise and kind:
His mouth rejects 'the flannel'
For he's too polite to mind.

He merely states politely,
Four times escaped from death
As he fought patrols that nightly
Missed him by a hairs-breadth.

The politician's mouth was thin
He's cross for the views he makes
Although they seem convincing
Have not the clout it takes.

The General's form of bravery
Says, "Attack, or all be lost,
We must oppose all slavery,
However high the cost."

The politician tries to show
Appeasement is the best:
The Bishop opts for "Yes and No"
And there, the matter, does rest.

DISSIDENT POEMS

"It is only Time that weighs upon our Hands,
It is only Time, and that is not material."

Sylvia Plath, 1963

Poem (Three Women)
Winter Trees.

THE GULAG ARCHIPELAGO

Oh, Gulag Archipelago
Haunting Isles of fear and sorrow,
Satanic demons here are bold
As in fierce fairy tales of old;
Where childhood's terror stricken eye
Sheds forth its tear with trembling sigh
When on early morning lighting
Printed page reveals … its writing,
Imagination wraps her cloak,
Eyes, laughing, dry their dismal soak.

This long lost world that could transform
An ogre grim to fairy form
Mocks down the years as dazed within
The grasp of perpetrated sin
They flee, great hordes; this human herd's
Existence now abhorréd word;
Whose children never will be born,
Whose bones unburied, lie forlorn.
The Author's talent is most rare
His plight to tell, their grief to share.

So soft, so musingly he speaks
His native language so repeats
The chosen word; each one so clear
It seems quite possible to fear
A likely Fate could cloud this land
Like ostrich safe with head in sand;
His luck has held, he's grown in size,
He early learned a lesson wise.
"Will blinded be forget the past,"
Quote Russian proverb, gravely cast.

"Life's breaking point is your arrest...
Incapable you take the test;
Your centre of the Universe
Is shattered at this word so terse.
Each bright or dull can only gasp
"Me, what for?" a million ask
As somersaulted from one state
They fail to notice till too late,
Or penetrate to understand
The Gulag Country's close at hand.

Above-you blinks fake circus moon
As unwiped jackboots stamp the room;
Dim the memory of the night,
"All's a mistake, they'll set things right."
Pale, trembling hands pack piece of soap;
What more to take to bolster hope?
Speed is the essence, nothing's clear
Haste as a weapon, fosters fear.
A witness sits in servile state,
He finds it hard to keep awake.

What follows next when you are gone
To dominate what was your home?
A crushing force like hungry beast
That hurls and rips, eats its fat feast;
Piles litter dumped like heap of bone
Dried in desolate desert home.
Here, jackal lips are smacked in joy
And victim treated like a toy.
There's nothing sacred in a search,
A child's small coffin once besmirched.

From your parched lips no single cry,
No Dissident's clear voice shouts, "Why?"
The Author's Tale tells solemn need,
Cries, "Two hundred million, heed."
One pale spring day on Baltic Sea
His guns surround the enemy.
All unsuspecting is unarmed
Intent so evil, was unwarned.
They strip him bare, star, board and belt
While Suite stood still, mute terror felt.

No thought of danger, letters send;
They read words written to his friends:
Brigade Commander spoke with weight,
"I wish you happiness," his Fate
United with a German shell,
Breathed equal death out here to spell.
His captors, S.M.E.R.S.H. have lost their way
As could not read the map's clear say.
Together they together go;
Him stifling closet grimly show.

The village Soviet decreed
It did not write out formal deed.
The people cast of simpler mould
They left no memoirs to unfold.
Deep in the permafrost they sank
Then wave on wave in sewers stank;
Pulped and pulsed poured sweat and blood
Piped, alternating ebb with flood.
Today some write and speak, recall
Positions high from which to fall.

Like anteater agile and young
All insects trap with sticky tongue;
Scoops in myriads heap on heap
Swept in one massive meal, to eat;
So Comrade Lenin duly wrote,
"Purge these insects," those who spoke
Against his Regime cruel and vile
Priests and nuns and monks on trial –
Generals, statesmen, all were shot,
Poor hostages were caught in plot.

All officers when sent en masse
From Rostov to Novocherkassk
Were battened down and hid from view
In silent barges by the crew.
They'd rose to fight the Civil War
Caught, were devoured by hungry maw.
There they sank in Caspian Sea
By The Isles of Solvetskey.
Or wrapt forever far from home
At Archangel in White Sea foam.

Great patience, patience was the trait
Non Party Members met their fate
As Bolsheviks allayed their fears
With stealthy method stretched through years.
Like grandiose game of solitaire
Invisible as winter's air;
Someone with cold far-seeing mind
Planned with neat hand to win and find
A card that lay three years on pile
Was softly moved and stored in file.

There is no antidote to quell
These servitors which life style spell
Greed for power, greed for gain;
Intense and avid they acclaim
Existence lived on lower sphere:
Putrefactions flourish here
Where bat and owl in silent flight
Pale executioners of night;
Capture by moonbeam harmless vole
Half blind and weak that strays from hole.

Let victim prove hostile intent,
Was interrogators evil bent.
Contact denied like hermit old
Who, kept at bay by wild beast bold
Crouched in cavern weak and pale,
His fossiled bones found light and frail.
Or searcher in the dark bowelled earth
Groping his path as fearing death.
When broken boulders block his way
In desperate fear can only pray.

With schoolchild's seven kopek pen
He weakly signed, gave in to them;
Was like a routine writ each day
For listed soap the ration pay
"Corrective Labour Camp, eight years,"
Each day spelt out in salty tears.
Defensive living we extolled
As roared with laughter, uncontrolled
Inside myself the truth I prise
"To live to not live, why survive?"

Mysterious as sleigh bells soft
Or nebulous as cloud aloft,
The Troika became Truine
And to their typist played a tune.
The O.S.O. did not condemn
Imposing penalty on them
Who kneeling to prevent escape
As fast unload from cruel freight.
By Polar Seas the Zeks were dying;
On May the first, Red Flags were flying.

A prisoner's life before each change
In steamy bath, ideas exchange.
Close to God's Paradise did seem
In emerald park of vivid green;
The air was fresh, the sparrows called
As 'Spring of Victory', recalled.
On the lowest form of being
The grim moustached Stalin, seeing
Grey millions floating in the rear
Like herring shoals in water clear.

"I've fifteen years," he laughed aloud,
Joy, like the sun disperses cloud
Burst from his dry constricted throat;
Aglow in haste to share the joke
As Jester in the King's grave court
Jingles his bells to make fine sport;
Cavorting in this world apart
His Fool's face covers breaking heart.
Absurdity worn like a gown
To play the role of happy clown.

As Universe holds countless stars
Hope marks their heart with minute scars.
Where penalty supreme is paid
Death's Angel, assignation made.
They file in reverence to pray
Past photographs, proud homage pay.
They sigh, they multiply, they curse
Mind overwhelmed forget the worst.
Like pilgrims trekking Holy Place
Dismiss the hazards hourly face.

Where fractured Time traps tortured Race
In Zone of Euclidian space
Invisible in freezing air,
Through thousand islands scattered, where
The Slaves have volume, substance, weight
From Bosphorus to Bering Strait.
White swans that wing the winter sky
Fan out not seen by naked eye;
Their camouflage is nature's way,
Protected here, does Man betray.

What Time and Time Past really are,
To trace internal state of star;
Conflicting force, steel bars, and soul.
To solve these mysteries his goal
Burns as soft halo of a saint;
Or glow-worm's gleam that glimmers faint.
Ill-fated lifelike futile moth
That circles flame, flies back and forth
To fall …   dark silence aids his dreams -
Know Spirit ruling all, supreme.

A PRISONER OF CONSCIENCE

In yards and stables in the village
Vibrant with desire, not pillage
Came the solemn trumpet sounding
Sound that set his glad heart pounding.
As camels honked and donkeys brayed.
With head upturned he hoped and prayed.
They told of faith in their own fashion,
Vibrant with desire and passion
This martial din merged with the roar
Within his breast with heart so sore.

In eagerness he found a place
As at his back the armed guards brace;
A kitchen corner where a bed
Of wooden crates cradled his head,
Became his home; no escorts walked
As on the streets loud speakers talked.
Told unexpected news, that first
Changed nothing in his life when thirst
And hunger were the norm
And purges swept through towns at dawn.

To accept his lot he was resigned
And exile Document was signed
With claustrophobic undertone
And complicated rules alone.
'In perpetuity', this brink
Could make a lesser spirit sink.
Veteran as he was of worse
Belik he praised, nor did not curse;
Once out of reach now bright and clean
Spacious and varied like a dream,

He made a vow that where he stood
With nothing owned but box of wood;
His ethics, conscience so demands
Obedience gives to man's commands.
Without support he was alone.
No friends save books as family gone.
Then, one fine day, a link was made
And foundations to a new life laid;
A kindred soul by fate produced
And counter ethic was induced.

This minor clerk was more than brave
To risk his life by act so grave.
And help him secure a teaching post
As if he recognised this ghost
This simple stressed and lonely man
Who stumbled here was part of plan
As laid down by the Universe.
'Subservience' to reject as cursed.
Spring scented air with smell of grass
Blew in from Steppe upon his class.

In old fur hat and worn-down heel
With hair turned dull but mind of steel;
He pivots strongly to oppose
Political or moral codes
That written for security
Ends steeped in depravity.
He found himself a little house
To live in safe as any mouse
That burrows in a bed of straw
Secure from sharpened feline claw.

Four tiny windows framed a face
At last at peace in its own place;
Tall chimney looming overhead
Looked down upon a road which read
No 10, Pioneer Street;
A pleasing name both real and neat,
Old stove he fed gave heat enough
Burned desert bush both hard and rough.
Small patchwork garden planned with care
Gave produce green and flowers fair.

Knowing, he felt the time was ripe
To free his powerful urge to write;
Save his memory from more pain
Commit to paper once again
Several factors were enough
To inhibit him, it was too rough
Too hardly won; subconscious fear
Imposed to stop his wish most dear.
He needed special kind of rest
To heal the wounds of his arrest.

His zeal was like a whirlwind blown
In whose fierce wake fruit seeds are sown;
Or lighting sharp behind dark cloud
With crashing chords that thunder loud.
Mysterious Cosmos was his theme
Held each child spellbound, as in dream:
While in his breast a monster clawed
Grinding in pain, vice like it pawed
As panther black and sleek at night
Captures its prey without a fight.

The future beckoned like a lamp
Whose single glow shines in a camp
Where soldiers sleep before a light
Brings peace and end of fight.
The gracious park that housed the sick
Contained acacias bright to pick.
Succulent grass fringed spreading oak
Whose shaded branches draped a cloak
Of fragrant leaves that danced and spun
In texture soft warmed by the sun.

Frail leggy foal with amber eyes
Called to its mare with plaintive cries;
White tennis balls flashed fast and free –
Black funeral's stately pace, decree.
On bamboo handles twirled above
Young fashioned women, meek as dove:
Parasols of swirling blue
Intoned with pink of every hue.
Diaphanous garments cling like wings
Of dragonflies, warm summer brings.

Exotic blossom's heady scent
Whose sweet or bitter odours lent
To his senses new dimension
And his soul's commitment, strengthen.
He found a silent place to wait
Through the ancient Golden Gate.
Felt the very depth of magic
In his life, both dear and tragic.
The simple peasants were the poor –
Like dusty sawdust strewn on floor.

These were the tortured drowning ones
Dazed and mute before the guns.
Pure tale he formed, each finished line
Marked stroke on stroke like etcher fine;
Or spider weaving subtle web
Picked clean of its imprisoned dead.
Meticulous with stubborn pace
Repairs its work of fragile lace.
Its form skeletal bare and white
Outlined against the winter light.

As waves eternal flow and ebb
When oceans cast ashore their dead;
Within a year he found his theme,
Portray a rhythm to things seen.
His images were spirit born
Crowding a mind already torn;
Tumbling as the salmon rise
Upstream while fighting for their prize.
He witness bore to prisoners' fate,
Discarnate figures at Hell's Gate.

The black procession shuffled slow;
In Goya nightmare pictured so.
In contrast bloomed the cherry tree
'Neath which he wrote for all to see.
Its mass of dainty pink tipped flowers
Dropped petals through the sunny hours.
His secret writings, undisclosed
Compressed as that sweet juice disposed
By eager bees that seldom rest
As honeycombs' clear nectar, press.

His inner world he did not change
As if in magician's castle, strange
Knew ancient Plato's pupils strolled
In Linden Park, ideas extolled;
Or, in Athenian olive grove
They spoke of death and life and love.
How conquered fear makes man sublime
In special moment caught in Time.
Now, lack of boots caused fear and fights
Where stars outshone by border lights.

'Christ's Passion vilified today',
His Lenten Letters told them "Pray"
Where hidden secrets of the heart
Lie as the roses' petals part
Ambrosial, whose perfume rare
Hovers in the summer air.
His faith in Christ glowed like the sun –
So Mankind's Laws of Life are run
On single course, to only cease
In clash of life and death … for peace.

ONE DAY IN THE LIFE OF IVAN DENISOVICH

In windowed glass, reflected, seen
Three lamps fling out their yellowed beam;
Where tallowed candles waxing clear
Burn on the blessed altar near.
Then priest benign his cassock takes
With head bowed, to the belfry makes;
And ancient church bells' holy sound
Clear, clangs across God's hallowed ground.
Here, hammer beats its hollow note -
At five o'clock grim message spoke.

The Leader spoke, bad news he told;
Their prayer, salvation from the cold.
All wait in fear to learn whose loss:
Not Alyosha, he took cross
And carried it, his daily bread
By faith alone, his prayer said.
But Shukhow, lying on his board
Knew sawdust mattress hid his hoard.
Mountains to move not yet his aim;
Just warmth and freedom from life's pain.

He listened low in cocooned lair
His buried form belied him where
White cobwebs spun like frozen lace;
Festooned huge hut's forbidding face.
Fresh morning laid her milky track,
Showed huddled forms like hummock's back
Thrown up in thousands where the mole
Industrious scoops earth from hole;
Blind in dark tunnel turns rough snout
Antenna like to root about.

When Tartar's face stared up at him
With levelled head hairless and thin
Like prairie dog in desert wide
Who bays with choking bark to hide:
But new moon shows his gleaming jaws,
Feet flitting fast on padded paws:
Or leaf that clothes a tender shoot
With buried deep tenacious root,
That rudely touched is blown by storm
Of Winter's gale, to lie forlorn.

"Do three day's penalty with work,"
The unfair punishment left hurt;
Protested for the sake of form
And clad in rags each garment torn,
Showed digits multiplied four times.
S850 in faded lines.
They hurried past high fence of wood
And frosted rail... new pole which stood
In sheltered spot to mark the cold
As milk white tube its rating told.

"There's a draught; you scum shut the door."
"You pig scrub down the guard room floor."
No lock up loomed his heart was gay;
With gloveless hands watched bucket sway
Above the thick ice coated well.
He did not note numb fingers swell
As barefoot on his knees he bends:
Work was a stick that has two ends -
For knowing ones your willing tool,
Eyewash was only for the fool.

"You can't compare millet with rice.
You, 850, I've told you twice,
Just make it moist and go, you skunk."
"Yes Citizen Chief," ... to empty bunk
Eat piece of bread, or report sick?
He had to make his mind up quick:
But first to mess-hall where the steam
Rose thick as bathhouse cut by stream
Of icy air ... sat at table
Measured skilly dished from ladle.

He moved his hat from shaven head,
Pulled spoon from boot, embossed, it said
'YST IZ MA_1944',
His bread he saved to later gnaw.
The putrid fish, none could disguise
He could not eat the floating eyes:
He sucked the bones and champed his teeth;
Searched black boiled cabbage underneath
For flesh on head and gill and tail,
Scraped skeleton of every scale.

Soft snow squeaked loudly underfoot
Leaked icy cold inside his boot.
The Bay was silent as a tomb
As eye slid o'er white ghostly room:
Not even minute mice could scratch
As killed by cat … no ticking watch.
So weak explorer of the North
Is awed by dazzling scene brought forth.
Bent sterile form faint figures wrote
Spaced out in lines, stroke upon stroke.

Thus Angel Gabriel might sit
Write down who's doomed for Hell's black pit:
Or who is saved to lie in bed
Three weeks in Heaven on clear soup fed.
Uneasily he felt his chin
Where, prickly as the hedgehog's skin
Fast stubble grew ... he thought again
This newest doctor cured all pain:
His first rate medicine was toil,
All who could stand could work the soil.

Confused with guilt he felt ashamed
As of some heinous crime was blamed.
"Why come so late, the list is done,
The evening is the time to come;
This morning's quota, two exempt,
Best go to work," so out he went:
Struck dumb with cold, emotions torn
Could not explain to man who's warm.
He slipped like shadow through the yard
Avoided rule, hat off to guard.

He coughed with pain as murky fog
Wreathed wretched form freed now to jog.
Like mummies bound from chin to eye,
With hearts aquake, the prisoners lie;
Few precious moments to forget
Await the order, "Out you get."
Across his bread heap sugar smooth,
He took long look, his heart to soothe.
How much short weight to make him ill,
He was too tired to cavil.

On twenty grams he did decide
One half to take and one to hide.
Inside his hat brim hidden deep
Was thread and needle, his to keep.
Barefoot he crawled to mattress end,
Stowed crust in rear then rent attend.
The Baptist read his Testament
From secret Book ... he joyous spent
This leisure time as honey bee
Sips nectar ... with felicity.

Like jackdaw, hides its jewelled hoard
Masked items miser like, he stored;
Fought the elements with fresh rag
Like tattered scarecrow newly clad.
In single file all ventured forth;
So cautious penguins of the North
Who rise from sea where graceful glide
On hostile land to slip and slide:
Bend bulky backs as low they shuffle
As bitter wind their footsteps muffle.

His numbers were in need of paint,
Guards locked you up if they were faint;
If too bright they warned and worried
So, to the ancient artist, hurried;
When hat he stroked with brushes fine
Anointed brow like priest benign.
As blew in glove-warmed fingers frail
Uncurled their form like frozen snail
Basks in the wintry sun to creep
Where fertile warmth awakes from sleep.

A prisoner's life is full of hurts,
They're stripping all of undershirts:
In charge is wolf like Volkovie.
Whose plaited whip drew blood to see.
Trapped, treasured heat escaped bare breast,
There is nothing but his soul in chest.
Like flock of sheep halt, all form fives
Five heads, five backs, ten legs besides;
Grey dogs bare teeth in baleful grin
And Tommy-guns press close to skin.

A prisoner's thought no longer free
As slashing wind made hard to see;
To stop his empty belly's beg
He thought of some strange news he'd read
A new craft, carpet painting paid
Enormous sums his wife had said.
But candidly he shunned the thought
In forty years he'd not been bought;
No teeth or hair yet held not grease
A palm or two to find his peace.

The sprawling maze held sun's red light
As columns halted at the sight
And guardhouse chimney belched grey smoke;
The Baptist smiled accepted yoke
In Dante's sad Fraternity
So lived souls in Purgatory.
From six watchtowers 'Parrots' perched
For warm corners, prisoners searched;
Like migrating swallows seek
Embossed soft an island creek.

In wadded trousers, found a seat;
Felt whetted edge of crust, how sweet
To chew with all your soul ... recall
Vast village meals, too much ... now small
Ambrosial morsel of black bread
Filled both his belly and his head.
Fetukaw the Jackal found
Fished from spittoons and on the ground
Fag ends he broke and filtered fine;
"Give us a drag," his constant whine.

As blood red sun climbed noonday sky
Days stood still yet years rolled by
Like static Earth on axis spin
With Moon and Stars encircling.
Five, caught by Hun, with one escaped
For food dead horses' hooves they scraped.
Truth, rewarded with false reason
Unfairly sentenced for high treason:
Like ant that flies from forest blaze
Flies back to base to burn, dismayed.

Some jabbed with picks the stone hard earth
Like woodpecker hacks trees' wide girth.
Some dragged cement on sledge by hand
Cleared snow, fetched water, carried sand;
Machine shop's gaping windows board
With trowel found in squirreled hoard.
Two men as three worked in straight row
All hidden well in cloak of snow.
Scrounged from pre-fabs, viewed behind,
Steered stolen roll of felt for blind.

Like zealous birds in early spring
In beaks small sticks and chips, will bring
Together gathered softly form
A tiny nest to keep them warm;
So prisoners hid small scraps to burn
And kindle ... keep the coal dust firm ...
Five hundred men booed, stiff with fear
So counted cattle when lost steer
After a frantic search is found -
Loud snort and stamp confined to pound.

The steaming mortar froze in frost
And petrified if left, was lost.
Like winded horse in chariot race
Each hauled and sweated, set a pace;
So straining leader of fierce pack
Of huskies heaving heavy sack
Whips at his mercy limping line
Reluctant pull to bank and climb.
Their team-mate shouted, "To the gate,
You're for the cells if listed late."

"A lucky day without a cloud."
"But for whose sake," he asked aloud.
An almost happy day, content
He built a wall, his illness went …
Ate meaty piece of sausage rare:
On hearing Alyosha's prayer
Asked, "Crave you freedom free from fears,
Time heavy weighed?" "Why all these tears
Apostle Paul told him, rejoice
Christ made imprisonment His choice."

HOPE AGAINST HOPE

Objectively, she donned a guise
Spelt naked truth, attacked the lies
Her pilgrim need thus made her say
"This I can do, this role I play."
Burdened by its saddened note
Glad, inexplicably, she wrote
Of liberation, humour, joy
'Luminous sadness' to employ.
Her ample spirit lent an air
Of triumph that dispelled despair.

Though opposition was most feared
One 'visitor of night' appeared
In stove pipe trousers smart and neat
Gave box of candy hard and sweet.
With skill and speed he searched the room,
This uninvited guest spelt doom
As vulture grim finds carrion's place,
Or hound that harassed hare does race
Against lost time, with feet of lead
And quickened heartbeat joins the dead.

Strict ritual deemed five men they take
For witnesses, two souls they fake.
To cover up their evil deed
As tiny hole in skull not bleed
On forehead high whose dome concealed
A massive brain, with blood congealed.
Their bodies search, a warrant hand
Like scavengers pick bones on sand.
Defenceless, as the tender doe,
He asks them, "Is it time to go?"

In Lubyanka every year
The corridors were signalled clear
But tall Chinese with bulging eye,
Amazed, was hustled out to die.
Her spine chilled, with fierce dread engaged
Her piercing look made guards enraged,
Was like a nightmare where grey ghouls
Rush piecemeal searching out for souls.
Holy terror, agonising,
Made her tremble, thus surmising.

"Our ancestors, dark death beguiled
Once under their grey mounds they smiled
Incense sweetly smelling spread,
And angelus deep tolled for dead.
From stones and belfries based on good,
Faint echoes float o'er field and wood
Now, churches peeling domes unblessed
Their rusty rib cage bears its breast;
And mocking boys bring knives to brawl
And on the altar, icons scrawl."

Cooped like a wild bird trapped in cage
Whose weary wings beat bars in rage
He suffered wishing time could cease,
Each fleeting moment measure peace:
He faced a future without hope,
As prisoner grasped a loop of rope
To finish that which has no taste
Not linger long, but die in haste;
Though promised miracles were done
Still heads were rolling, one by one.

Incapable of any guile
The truth he answered at his trial
'Preserve but isolate', expect,
They knew first draft of fatal text
Sickening method was superb,
Irrational force … no harsh word
If nothing left, then both must scream,
To prove alive, to break the dream.
The right to open doors, draw breath,
If this were lost, then welcome death.

His poems piled like mountain's snow
Pyramids rose pink aglow
Then no more seen, consumed as flame
Of summer sun melts it to rain.
Instinctively she formed a plan,
To salvage manuscript, not man
Memories perish with the flesh
That creeps like rabbit mauled in mesh:
When stoat stares at its stricken prey,
Relentless long through night and day.

He had one final loathsome task
Write 'hymn of praise', submit a mask
So give immunity to wife,
Meanwhile relinquishing his life
Heads, mounds of heads, he was dismayed,
The balance of his mind was swayed:
Like matrix seethed, cancelled 'the Ode',
Antagonistic to its code
As charmer in the snake pit dares
To milk off venom for his wares.

Poems assessed at current rate
Their static line whispered his fate
Sober, he viewed approaching end,
No privacy to help his trend.
His 'sweet voiced labour', he composed
Like seed to its ripe fruit transposed
Or diver on aquatic bed,
Who prays the silent words, unsaid.
Will oyster's tight seamed shell uncurl,
He, delving deep, discovers pearl?

Grim ogres in their ivory tower
Outlawed by their greed for power
Show facts of life to undermine,
In fundamental rule of time.
Indoctrination's natural aim,
Gives these satanic monsters, fame.
This arrogance from such a height
Made man revolt, and need to fight,
Extermination is his fate,
Were only language of the State.

STARS OF BURMA NOTES

Japan entered the Second World War in December 1941 with an attack on the United States Pacific Fleet's base at Pearl Harbour in Hawaii. The Japanese conquered Indo-China easily but greater victories were won in Malaya and Singapore. The Dutch East Indies and the Western Pacific were then added to their control and Australia was threatened.

The Japanese plan was to invade Burma to take control of the Burma Road, the supply route for Nationalist China, so that cutting off this lifeline would facilitate conquering all of China. Also possession of Burma would lead them into India and supposedly easy victory. Entering Burma from Thailand the Japanese quickly captured Rangoon and took control of the Burma Road.

According to Winston Churchill, our Prime Minister at the time, our first Imperial obligation of the Second World War was to defend India from the Japanese invasion by which it seemed it was already menaced as this task bore a decisive relation to the whole war. To leave four hundred million of His Majesty's Indian subjects, to whom we were bound in honour, to be ravaged and overrun, as China had been by the Japanese would have been a deed of shame. Also to allow the Germans and Japanese to join hands in India or the Middle East involved a measureless disaster to the Allied cause.

Then began the 'Burma Campaign' in which the Allied forces fighting in Burma were the most multi-national and multi-racial in the whole of the war; they included American and British Air Squadrons and soldiers from British, Indian, African, Australian, New Zealand, Canadian, American, Chinese, Burmese and Gurkha armies.

The Anglo American command of the air was decisive and on May 3rd 1945 the long struggle with Burma ended. On May 9th Winston Churchill telegraphed the Supreme Commander sending his most "heartfelt congratulations upon the culminatory victory at Rangoon of his Burma Campaign." He said that, "the hard fighting at Imphal and Kohima in 1944 prepared the way for the brilliant operation, conducted over a vast range of territory which have crowned the exertions of the South East Asia Command in 1945: despite the diminution and disappointments you and your men have done all and more than your directive required."

"In honour of these great deeds of South East Asia Command His Majesty the King has commanded that a special decoration the 'Burma Star' should be struck and the ribbon will be flown out to you at the earliest moment."

This long poem, the *Stars of Burma*, written in short four-line verses is my way of tribute to 'A Forgotten Army'.

On hearing the death of General Orde Wingate (see *Operation Thursday*) Churchill said, "with him a bright flame was extinguished."

I remember walking in the countryside outside the city of Oxford in the early days after the Second World War and my feet touched a solid piece of dirty upright concrete covered in earth and grass. I bent down to examine it and read this inscription: *In memory of Orde Wingate,* then followed some obscured lettering. I felt it was amazing that I should have stumbled on this little monument and wondered if Churchill was responsible. It was in a beautiful wild spot on the edge of a very darkly wooded tree area stretching far into the distance.

WAR POEMS NOTES

Winston Churchill's War Declaration

I was training in Hammersmith Hospital to be a SRN when I heard this speech.

Winston Churchill (A Tribute)

"Churchill's supreme achievement, amounting to a miracle was to turn the British in 1940, within a few weeks and single handed, once again into a brave people, and by doing so to save Western civilisation."

Recollections of a Rebel – Lord Boothby 1978

"Historians are apt to judge War Ministers less by the victories achieved under their direction, than by the political results that flowed from them. Judged by that standard, I am not sure I shall be held to have done very well."

Churchill's statement after the war to Lord Boothby.

"I have said that from 1935-1939, the political leaders of this country were, with the exception of Winston Churchill, and Leo Amery, frightened men."

Lord Boothby

This poem is my own tribute to a great leader. Living my early life in the shadow of Winston Churchill, a great statesman, I felt I really knew him personally. I heard all his speeches on the wireless, and with Nelson, he remains, in my memory, indestructible.

Sixty years on I read an article in the *Sunday Times* dated May 1st 2005, the week of the General Election and the 60th anniversary of the end of the Second World War. It was titled 'Can we trust our leaders to lie for us?' One phrase stands out for me with great clarity 'Hitler was defeated by English poetry'.

Winston Churchill loved poetry; he quoted Tennyson once and paid homage to Rupert Brooke (see *Poem Tree* notes). He also quoted lines from Byron's *Childe Harold* to President Roosevelt and lines of Pope came into his head when at a meeting with Mr Stimson, the American

Secretary of War. It was Winston Churchill's poetical choice of words in his speeches that inspired the fighting spirit in this country to victory according to the article, 'Trusting our leaders to lie means believing that on the bigger things they are, like the philosopher king, in contact with the naked unadorned truth.'

Early in the Second World War Churchill convinced the sceptical British public of some great truths by his brilliant speeches: that we had to fight Hitler and that this was 'a duty that lay beyond all expediency'; we might die and be defeated but to die for this cause was better than to live without having fought.

The article continues, 'I think the great truth of Churchill's words sprang from something that our present leaders simply do not have – a coherent, justificatory myth of their role in the world. Churchill had a mystical, poetic belief in the land of England and it was this that gave his words their sacrificial intensity and, in the event, their truth.' So Hitler was defeated by English poetry and Churchill could have told us anything he liked for we would have known that his words were noble and we would have trusted him.

Black Dogs of the World (for Lotte)

Edward Storey, the poet, prompted me to submit this poem to *The Month* and it was published in an edition of this magazine. I dedicated the poem to Lotte Kramer and received a very kind letter from Lotte. Lotte is well known for her Holocaust poems, as she is a Holocaust survivor.

Fragment

After the Second World War I returned to Berlin to visit my daughter. I ordered a taxi at 11pm to take me to the Olympic Stadium where Hitler, as leader of the Nazi Party, gave his speeches, rallying the population to join his party of war and destruction. I sat on the nearest seat I could to the area where I had seen Hitler on the Pathe War News in the cinema at home under a glowing almost red harvest moon. It felt like the finish of a very long and tragic play now ended and the final curtain was lowered at last. The taxi then came to collect me and I slowly came back to earth, and left.

The Survivor

War survivors are mostly very reticent; the pain and hurt of their experiences goes too deep for words.

Desert Rat (7th Armoured Division)

These men endured appalling conditions in the Western Desert. Mostly they remember the sand which covered everything and the flies which were everywhere, unremitting and relentless. The fighting in the desert they do not mention.

The Sniper

I read about a Norfolk gamekeeper who was so quick on the trigger he was stationed behind enemy lines on his own to pick off persistent snipers who were causing havoc to our troops. I imagined him alone, foraging for food, trying to sleep, keeping well hidden; and saluted this brave soldier in my poem.

Normandy Beach

This poem is written in memory of a young doctor I knew who trained at 'Barts' and who had French nationality. I heard he had been killed, and I remembered his gaiety and how he had won a Gold Medal for Fencing in the Olympic Games before the war.

They Too

I read the American writer Samuel Hynes' book *Flights of Passage* and sent my poem *They Too* to him on an airmail letter. He wrote from London a very constructive letter, which cheered me tremendously. He is Professor of Literature at Princeton, a leading American university, so his words "You can be proud of *They Too*" were most encouraging. Many of his friends were reported missing when he trained in the American Air Force as a very young man at the beginning of the Second World War.

Remembrance Day

I remember my friends and relatives killed in the 1939-1945 War. The irony was that my first child was born during the Battle of Britain with Spitfire bullets hitting the flat lead roof of the building in which I was living in Wimbledon while looking after boys from Wimbledon College who were marooned there, their contemporaries were fighting above their school and homes and giving their lives, average age 19 years.

For the Valentines

I sat next to an ex-Tank Commander at a Burma Star Reunion dinner and he told me about the Valentines, and a tank called Willie Boy. I sent the poem to the Tank Museum at Bovington Camp, Dorset and was thrilled to hear from the Display Department that they had it copied and would frame it and hang it in the Museum.

War

Reactions to this event are turbulent and emotional.

47th Brigade, Burma

Dedicated to those men who fell by the wayside and were taken prisoner, especially Fusilier Dunn. This soldier was especially brave and this poem is for him.

Escape

This poem was written for the Royal Air Forces Escaping Society.

Question

This poem poses the question who wins and who loses in the days of technical warfare. The Germans built more submarines in 1944. In the final count British and British Controlled Forces destroyed 500 out of 632 submarines known to have been sunk at sea by the Allies. It was written when Nimrods and Shackeltons were in the combat zone.

The Promise

For all the broken promises war inevitably brings.

Katyn, 1940

This poem is dedicated to the brave Polish Officers who were so cruelly murdered, and whose bodies were discovered after the war buried in a forest. The monument is erected to them in London in tribute to their memory.

War Songs

These were a great morale boost to the soldiers, and also enjoyed by all the civilians who sang them in their working places, in factories and on the land.

Absolute

I remember the total shock the whole nation felt when news came over the wireless that a massive bomb had been dropped on Japan. It did successfully bring the Japanese war leaders to surrender and saved the lives of many Allied soldiers, but nevertheless, it was at an unimaginable cost of lives together with massive destruction of buildings.

The illustration is a photograph of a mustard tree; I read that the largest one in the world is in Palestine.

I sent this poem to Hutchinsons in April 1970 and received a letter in return from the Poetry Department saying that they "found it very interesting and if I should feel stimulated to write any prose of novel length, we would be interested to see it." I feel that maybe these stories about each poem are, in a way, my story.

The Diary (Anne Frank)

Young people today may not have heard of Anne Frank. This poem tries to explain what it was like for her shut up for years in an attic, hiding from the Nazis and discovered by them just before the liberation. She was sent to a concentration camp where she died of typhus. This poor child was so brave, so innocent, words are hard to find that are tribute enough to her suffering. Her diary was found after the war, hidden under the floorboards in her attic home in Holland, and has since been the subject of books and films.

The Sea Shall Not Have Them

This is a poem about ships being lost at sea by enemy action. Some of my friends worked plotting the movements of ships from secret bunkers. In the whole of the war 91 merchant ships were taken on the Arctic route. The Merchant Navy lost 829 lives while the Royal Navy paid a still heavier price: two cruisers and seventeen other warships were lost and 1,840 officers and men died.

The Tanks

These weapons are fearsome, and take on a special meaning in a war. I have met some of the men who manned them and they are indeed 'special', amazingly courageous.

Battle of Britain

In Winston Churchill's Victory Broadcast, as Prime Minister, on May 13th 1945 he stated that in July, August and September 40-50 squadrons of British fighter aircraft in the Battle of Britain broke the teeth of the German Air Force at odds of seven or eight to one. He continued, "In our island 46 millions of people had to import half their daily bread and all the materials needed for peace or war."

The young men who took part in the Battle of Britain were truly heroes of the highest order, many were my friends and they are remembered with gratitude and love.

Dawn Raid

I remember waking up and looking out of my bedroom window and seeing the planes in formation flying into the sunrise.

Truth

The unbelievable record of the Holocaust defies description; the work of the Devil. The bread and wine is symbolically biblical.

War Widow

These brave women remember their husbands as always young and loving. There are cherished faded photographs on mantelpieces showing a precious image captured in time.

Dunkirk

This also I wrote on my 75th birthday, 4th September 1991. As the Second World War broke out around my birthday I always recall these times of war.

A very good friend of mine, who fought in the whole of the war, bought a small fishing boat called *Lazy Days* which had been used by its fisherman owner to rescue soldiers trapped on the beach at Dunkirk. Inside on one of the cabin walls was a brass plaque stating this episode.

We drank our wine with a toast to these heroic men each evening at sunset as we remembered them. The snapshot shows one of the ex-Wimbledon College boys having tea on the terrace. He had recently been evacuated from Dunkirk.

Sons

This poem was inspired by the news of a mother whose three sons were killed in action in World War II

Memory (War Bride)

So many war weddings ended in failure due to the dramatic circumstances of war which entailed long separations and isolation and many men returned to find their whole future changed.

The Bomb

There is much disputing over the manufacture of nuclear bombs and indeed all technology used in today's defence programmes.

Chinese Girl

I read of a beautiful Chinese girl who smuggled food to a Prisoner of War in Singapore. She refused to keep the food for herself and took no payment, and it would have meant torture and death for her if she had been caught. She herself was near starvation and the British P.O.W. never forgot her, and when he returned after the war tried to find her but to no avail.

Do not Consort with Death (for Mussolini)

Mussolini was a Fascist leader in Italy during the Second World War. I wrote this poem after seeing a T.V. programme showing a play by Thomas Mann in which the actors were portraying an Italian audience. The play was set in a small Italian village and the main character, a magician, cracked his whip and exhorted the audience to carry out his commands.

Sark Poems

I have a grandson who was born in Sark, the smallest of the Channel Islands. His grandfather regaled me with tales of the occupation, when the Germans seized the island during the Second World War. He told of desperate food shortages, undercover operations, the bravery of his fellow islanders and also how the enemy was often outwitted. German soldiers were found at the foot of raised terrain around the bay; apparently they had been killed during the night due to an 'unfortunate accident'. The defence given by the islanders was that they were ignorant about the geography of the island and fell to their deaths, but my father-in-law knew differently. I wrote these poems when I returned after peace was restored.

Sea Song (Malta)

I was having a picnic by the sea on the beautiful island of Malta. My daughter Celia and her small son were with me and I fell asleep. I dreamt about Shakespeare's play *The Tempest*; inspired by the beautiful views around I wrote this poem.

During World War II this island was so heroic that the special medal 'The George Cross' was conferred on the island of Malta in 1942. The George Cross is awarded for acts of courage in circumstances of extreme danger. I met a widow there who had her late husband's medal.

Birth

This poem was written to describe how nature redresses the balance after there has been great destruction including a tremendous loss of life due to war.

The London Blitz

One night the famous musical centre, The Queen's Hall, London, was destroyed by fire in an air raid. There was a huge yellow glow on the horizon, and the sky was alight for miles around. The poem is after Robert Browning's poem *Love among the Ruins.*

The British sense of humour was always a great morale boost in war-time, especially the wit and spark of the Cockneys, as people from the East End of London were called. During World War II, King George VI and Queen Elizabeth visited this badly bombed area of London. At the same time Buckingham Palace had received a hit from a bomb and the Guard's Chapel at Windsor a direct hit which killed 6 soldiers. Queen Elizabeth was quoted as saying, "Yes my home has also suffered." It was a great morale boost at the time, especially as their Majesties stayed in England all through the war with the two little princesses.

Operation Torch (Rock of Gibraltar)

This poem illustrates 'Operation Torch' during the Second World War. The Rock of Gibraltar had a great concentration of aircraft and the whole isthmus was crowded with machines. Gibraltar had been prepared for a siege since 1939 and its greatest contribution to the War was the development of its new airfield. Its role as an important part in the operations, both military and political, for the plan to invade and occupy French North Africa – 'Operation Torch', was that of a garrison fort. As Churchill said, "it was like fitting jewels into a bracelet". I use the simile 'jigsaw' in the poem. The dragon is the emblem of England, the monkey represents France and the gorilla in a tree symbolises the Rock of Gibraltar.

The Healing Hop

During the Second World War a very close friend of mine, training for her SRN at Hammersmith Hospital, was on duty when she had some terrible news. Her entire family: mother, father, brother, sister, aunt and uncle were all killed outright by a bomb dropped by a German plane on its way back to Germany after an air raid on London. The bomb made a direct hit on the air raid shelter in the garden where they had all spent the night. This happened in the county of Kent, renowned for its hop fields; I remember going with her to their funeral and seeing six coffins. She was only 21 years old and went back to duty on the wards the following day.

Patriotism

This poem is written in the style of Rupert Brooke after seeing a poetry competition. The entries were modern and quite different from my version which could appear old fashioned in comparison.

A Legend (HMS Victory)

I had just had one of my six knee operations and needed an outing after long days in plaster. So I booked a local coach trip to see HMS Victory as I had never done so and Nelson was my hero. I had a lovely day and as I was disabled a young rating was told to help me over the ship. I wrote this poem when I got home and was thrilled to receive a kind letter from C.P. Addis Lieutenant Commander, Royal Navy who thanked me for my 'beautiful poem'.

I include this poem, for although Nelson's victory at Trafalgar did not take place during the 20th century, this year, 2005, sees the celebrations of the 200th anniversary of Trafalgar Day.

All Quiet on the Western Front

Written in memory of my uncle who was killed in World War I.

Feet of Gold (Sonnet for Wilfred Owen)

Wilfred Owen and his brother Harold played as children in a meadow of buttercups where golden pollen collected on Wilfred's boots. Harold pointed to them and cried, "Look, Wilfred, you have golden feet." Later Wilfred was to remember these words, so apt and poignant and my sonnet is about this incident.

Heroes (November 11th, Remembrance Day)

Two minutes silence, the Queen at the Cenotaph and the poignant picture each year on the television made me write my own epitaph.

Old Contemptibles

The yearly journey made to the war graves in France by the British Survivors inspired this poem.

War Sonnet (for the Tommies)

This is in memory of ordinary British soldiers, who fought in both World Wars, and were affectionately known as "Tommies".

The Red Poppy

This flower grew profusely in the fields of France, and fabric copies were manufactured in thousands and sold by the British Legion to raise funds every year on November 11th, Armistice Day.

Poem Tree

This poem is for Rupert Brooke, war poet who died on April 23rd 1915. When the Admiralty was informed of the death, Winston Churchill sent an obituary to *The Times.*

In World War II when flying over Greece on a fact-finding mission; Churchill asked the pilot to fly a loop over the island of Skyros to pass over the tomb of Rupert Brooke.

Brooke died from of amoebic dysentery, according to an old biography I have of him, and one of the symptoms of this disease is blood in the stools (crimson cloak) and the drugs administered include belladonna commonly known as the poisonous deadly nightshade.

In 1905 in his last term at Rugby Brooke wrote to a friend, St John Lucas, "only my present happiness is so great that I fear the jealous gods will requite me afterwards with some terrible punishment, death perhaps - or life!" Quoting from a fragment of a last elegy by Brooke, "He is the silence following great words of peace."

Brainwashing (Czech Pavilion, Expo 70)

I wrote this after reading an article by Eric Newby in *The Observer* about this exhibition. I sent him a copy of *Brainwashing* and he wrote back to me saying how moving he had found my poem.

Tin Man

After watching a film on TV about the Italian painter Giorgio de Chirico, who was a major inspiration to the Surrealists, I sent this poem to Christopher Peacock of Southern TV. His reply was very encouraging.

War Photographer

This was written on seeing a stark war picture of the Vietnam War in *Life Magazine.*

The Letter

Solzhenitsyn had cancer diagnosed while he was imprisoned and was treated in hospital. I read some of his books and this is a poem to pay tribute to him. The Dissident Poems are also tributes to him and his work.

I.R.A.

A pupil at the college where my husband taught became a young priest, and his parents were friends of our family in Wimbledon during the Second World War. He was tortured and killed by the I.R.A. and his body was only found much later on.

Cornelia

I went to Berlin when it was divided into Zones to visit my eldest daughter who was married with two young children and was unhappy with her sergeant husband. I took my four-year-old daughter with me on the troop train through Check Point Charlie, where we stopped in a tunnel while our passports were examined by the Russians. We went on a coach tour to a Garden of Remembrance in East Berlin and it was like a scene in a technicolour movie: the concrete statues, the red star in the building, full of paper wreaths, and the Russian soldiers on guard in the rain with their slanting eyes and rifles at the ready. My daughter had to go to the lavatory, and when we came out our group had already reached our coach which nearly left without us.

I learned later that people were smuggled out of the Eastern Sector; which was grey and miserable, to the lights and gaiety and freedom of the British Zone in the coach we were using for sightseeing. When I read about Cornelia, a young German violinist, getting caught as she tried to escape from the East in the boot of a car, I remembered the incident and the atmosphere.

Falkland Sailor

This is a little poem which is a tribute to the men of the War in the Falklands.

The Barrier (Equador)

This is a sad comment on the suffering of women and children in wartime.

Aeriel 5

I was in hospital with my leg in plaster, and was in some pain. I listened to a talk on my radio headphones as I was drifting off to sleep. The programme was about stars and satellites and this poem came into my head. During World War II photographic reconnaissance using satellites played a major part in military intelligence and has since continued to be of great importance.

Toss a Coin in a Fountain (War Poets Remembered)

This also I wrote while in plaster and in much pain in hospital. It consists of quotations from war poets woven into my own poem about vivisection. There was a great outcry over the use of animals for experiments and I clearly remember anti-vivisection posters showing a terrified cat. I love cats and I can still see this in my mind's eye. However, lives were saved in the war with the discovery of anti-malaria drugs and later penicillin. It is an emotive subject open to much fierce debate.

Rudolph Hess

I remember hearing on the wireless (as the radio was called then) that an important henchman called Rudolph Hess had taken a small plane and defected from Hitler's Nazi Party and flown to Scotland. He was imprisoned by the British, and then, after the Nuremberg trials of war criminals subsequently incarcerated in a German prison for the rest of his life. Churchill felt he was a medical and not a criminal case and should be regarded as such. When I read about this man, so old and frail, being guarded day and night, a lone captive in a grim castle in Germany, I wondered if perhaps laws should not always be meted out indefinitely.

Company

This is a funny little poem that came into my head on my 75th birthday.

Hostage

Television today shows graphic pictures of people taken hostage and the terror and suspense of their plight. Before this, as with John McCarthy and Terry Waite, there were long years of silence as to their fate. It is those feelings of outrage and helplessness this crime engenders that makes it so unbearable. This poem is an effort to try to understand 'hostage taking'.

Gulf Crisis (Panel)

The war with Iraq to topple Saddam Hussein has been condemned by some and applauded by others. A stalemate has arisen due to insurgents and although Saddam Hussein has gone, it is an uphill struggle to get the process of democracy working fully in Iraq. I made these comments after watching a panel on the television discussing the crisis.

DISSIDENT POEMS NOTES

In pre-glasnost Russia, as in other autocratic states, dissidents demonstrated against the official party line and advocated a more open, democratic and humanitarian approach to life. Dissidents were sent into exile, put in prison or labour camps or incarcerated in mental institutions. It wasn't until the late 1980s when the Soviet leader Gorbachev began liberalising various aspects of Soviet life, lifting bans on censorship and opening up Soviet relations with the West that the number of dissidents fell.

Sakharov, the Russian scientist whose research produced Russia's first hydrogen bomb, was a supporter of the new reform programme. He realised that research cannot occur in a vacuum and that there are moral issues that should take precedence over scientific inquiry even if it requires some personal sacrifice.

Having seen the destruction caused by the hydrogen bomb he campaigned for nuclear disarmament, human rights and freedom of speech and thought in the USSR. He received the Nobel Peace Prize in 1975. In 1980 he was arrested due to his outspoken comments about Soviet action in Afghanistan and sent into exile at Gorky, where he was isolated from his friends and family and persecuted by the KGB.

Solzhenitsyn was imprisoned for his anti-Stalin comments. His books are semi-autobiographical and highly critical of the system. *One Day in the Life of Ivan Denisovich*, written in 1962 concerns the labour camps under Stalin. In writing *The Gulag Archipelago* about ten years later he exposes the whole Soviet camp network. This led to his expulsion from the Soviet Union in 1974.

Recently the grandson of an officer of the NKVD secret police opened 'The Shield and the Sword' a KGB themed restaurant, illustrating a recent revival of interest in Stalin in Russia. Impoverished and disillusioned Russians are now warming towards Joseph Stalin, the dictator whom Western historians blame for the death of millions of Soviet citizens during his bloody purges. Responsible for turning the Soviet Union into a feared but respected superpower, a recent poll has shown that half of all Russians interviewed consider Stalin a wise leader, while one in four said they would vote for him if he were standing for office today. Statements glorifying Stalin can now be heard among those born long after his death in 1953, but there are still plenty of Russians for whom the wounds of 50 years ago have scarcely healed.

Sergei Kovalev, a dissident, who spent 10 years in Soviet gulags, forced labour camps, thinks Stalin was a criminal and is appalled to hear that people are seriously considering erecting statues to him. As for Stalin's contribution during the Second World War, Kovalev ascertains he was so cruel that he branded Soviet soldiers who survived Nazi concentration camps as traitors and sent them to their deaths in the gulags.

The vital role played by the Soviet Union in smashing Nazi Germany, with the loss of 27 million people, during the Second World War remains a huge source of pride in Russia.

I read many books on Russia while I was in hospital because I had been in Berlin when it was divided into sections and was struck by the contrast between the French, British, American Zones and the Russian Zone; the former bright and affluent, the latter grey and dismal, depressing. Here was concrete evidence; also I have lived to see the Berlin Wall come down and the fall of Communism. So I feel to have made a record to describe the dreadful treatment many brave Russians were subjected to is my small way of remembering their suffering.

Hope Against Hope, is based on the book by Mrs Osip Mandelstam, *Hope Against Hope, And Every Killing is a Treat* written in 1965. It is a ballad dedicated to her husband, the late exiled Osip Mandelstam.

The Dissident Poems are ballads humbly dedicated to Mrs Sakharov and all the brave wives and families of dissidents throughout the world.

ILLUSTRATIONS

ILLUSTRATIONS (Continued)

Page

ILLUSTRATIONS (Continued)

Page

REGIMENTAL INSIGNIA

Back Cover – Clockwise

14th Army

17th Indian Division

5th Indian Division

23rd Indian Division

11th East African Division

36th British Division

81st West African Division

2nd British Division

The 'Chindits'

23rd Indian Corps

82nd West African Division

15th Indian Corps

25th Indian Division

4th Indian Corps

26th Indian Division

7th Indian Division